THE REFRACTIVE THINKER®

AN ANTHOLOGY OF DOCTORAL WRITERS

VOLUME XVII

Managing a Cultural Workforce
The Impact of Global Employees

Edited by **Dr. Cheryl A. Lentz**

THE REFRACTIVE THINKER® PRESS

The Refractive Thinker®: An Anthology of Higher Learning Vol XVII: Managing a Cultural Workforce: The Impact of Global Employees

The Refractive Thinker® Press
http://www.RefractiveThinker.com
https://Twitter.com/DrCherylLentz
https://www.Facebook.com/RefractiveThinker/

Books are available through The Refractive Thinker® Press at special discounts for bulk purchases for the purpose of sales promotion, seminar attendance, or educational purposes. Special volumes can be created for specific purposes and to organizational specifications. Please contact us for further details.

Library of Congress Control Number: 2013945437

Volume ISBN   978-1-7329382-4-3
               *Kindle and electronic versions available

Refractive Thinker® logo by Joey Root; The Refractive Thinker® Press logo design by Jacqueline Teng; cover design and production by Gary A. Rosenberg.

Printed in the United States of America

10 9 8 7 6 5 4 3 2 1

Contents

Testimonials

Brian Jud

Executive Director of the Association of Publishers for Special Sales, author of 14 books including *How to Make Real Money Selling Books*
http://www.bookmarketingworks.com/

Authors always want to know the latest out-of-the-box strategy to sell more of their books. *The Refractive Thinker*® series adopts this innovative-thinking approach, so you can get your doctoral research out of academia and into the hands of those who need it. This volume, regarding the impact of global employees in managing a cultural workforce, is a particularly good example of how to make that happen. There is no need to go it alone. Join your colleagues on a journey in search of creative and unique solutions as you navigate the landscape of business.

Jeanne Alford

Executive Director, Sudden Cardiac Arrest Association
www.suddencardiacarrest.org

This *Refractive Thinker®* series edition focused on managing workplace culture is a gem, a veritable MBA-in-a-flash. Collecting research findings, understanding research implications, and applying this knowledge is presented in a straightforward and practical manner. I specifically appreciated the Academic Entrepreneur chapter summaries provided by Dr. Cheryl Lenz. These summaries present the problem, pertinent questions, and conclusions in a way that further clarifies the authors' findings and how to apply them in the real world. Every CEO and their staff should have this as a required resource in their office.

Seema Giri, PMP

Award-winning Author, International Speaker, and Transformational Coach
http://www.seemagiri.com

In what I have seen in my 20 years of entrepreneurship, travelling globally and interacting with nearly 100,000 people, culture is one of the most important aspects of running a business whether big or small. *The Refractive Thinker®* series offers powerful insight of how to build cultures within the global economy. The inclusion of academia perspectives can be the next level resource to an MBA graduate. The anthology format is the perfect way to gain insights from the immense experiences of the doctoral contributors.

Olivia Parr-Rud, MS

Data Scientist, Bestselling and Award-winning author, and Corporate Love Ambassador
LoveMakeItYourBusiness.com

To thrive in today's fast-paced, high-tech, global economy, companies must understand and adapt to the unique needs in managing culture and the impact on the global workforce. *The Refractive Thinker*® series offers powerful, practical insights and strategies for navigating our increasing complex business landscape. The blend of academic rigor with real world applications through the lens of refractive thinking strategies provides unique, cutting-edge solutions important to business governance. *The Refractive Thinker*® *Vol XVII: Managing a Cultural Workforce: The Impact of Global Employees* is a potent addition to this series. Every business should make this entire series a staple in their corporate library.

*"Education is not the learning of facts,
it's rather the training of the mind to think."*
—ALBERT EINSTEIN

*"Education is the most powerful weapon
which you can use to change the world.'*
—NELSON MANDELA

The Power of the Connection
With the Universe

*"To this day, whenever I make it "out of the back," behind
the breaking waves, I offer a little prayer of gratitude—for that
experience, for that partnership with the universe."*
—BRIAN SMITH, AUTHOR OF *BIRTH OF A BRAND*

Business is about being open to possibilities, as well as to
the gifts that the universe offers. The secret is how you can
be creative and successful while *also* being true to yourself. We
are all creative, the challenge is learning to put that creativity to
work; this takes the power of learning.

Remember, you can't give birth to adults.

Business is about learning about people and ourselves along
the way. It doesn't matter whether the product is a new shoe, a
new device, or a new idea, every new paradigm follows the same
growth curve, from conception to adulthood. Whether raising a
child or an entrepreneur, the process is remarkably similar—both
take hard work and determination. We have to navigate through
our expectations, unshakeable optimism, and grinding endurance
in the face of unforeseen setbacks

Through the journey of UGG boots and building a billionaire
brand, my business philosophy emerged, crystallizing into what I
call Wisdom Points learned along the way. As shared in my book,
The Birth of a Brand: The Unlikely Start-up Story of the Billion

Dollar Brand, one thing I realized is that who you are in business is who you are in life, and when you act with integrity, stay true to your ethics, and just treat everyone with simple respect, you'll be successful, but more importantly, you'll be happy.

This Refractive Thinker® series is about being open to possibilities in research to find the successful way through business (and life!). Refractive thinkers are all about thinking differently regarding the need for course corrections in research; they understand that business principles have not changed, one simply continues to build on knowledge learned, always willing to go that extra mile to ask *what if* or *why not.* Thinking is not just in or out of the box. Refractive thinkers think *beyond* the box as scholars who understand the power of creating a vision; the way forward is one of persistence and above all patience. Answers will come, but in time and in partnership with others. Trust the process and trust your partners.

Join me to learn more about research behind the importance of culture, in the focus of the next volume in this award winning series. Partner with these doctoral scholars as they provide their research about the importance of people and collaboration of global partners and organizational vision. Learn to see the world through their eyes, yet still embracing the wisdom and counsel from the experiences of organizations and brands that came before them.

For the scholars of this *Volume XVII: Managing a Cultural Workforce: The Impact of Global Employees,* their missions are many. Topics in this volume include learning about what attracts investors, the effect of organizational vision, the organizational citizen, ensuring prosperous knowledge, employee engagement, importance of cross cultural competencies, the advantages of diverse teams, the importance of leadership and how it impacts culture, and the importance of being able to discuss the undiscussables. The thread that links all of us together is that successful leaders, business owners, and entrepreneurs believe they can make a difference to help others.

Believe in the power of the universe, the power of partnerships, and the power of you. Each of us should work to be successful and happy, but having given it our best shot, we must sit back and enjoy both what we have and what we've created, no matter how it turns out. The secret is in the relationships and friends we have developed along the way, the true fulfillment of an entrepreneur's dream.

Sincerely,
Brian Smith
Speaker, Author of *The Birth of a Brand*
brian@uggfounder.com
www.uggfounder.com

UGG FOUNDER
BRIAN SMITH

Preface

Welcome to the award winning Refractive Thinker® Doctoral Anthology Series. We are thrilled to have you join us for the 19th volume in the series (Vol II was published 3 times), *The Refractive Thinker®: XVII: Managing a Cultural Workforce: The Impact of Global Employees.* Join us as we continue to celebrate the accomplishments of doctoral scholars from around the globe.

Our mission continues to be to get research off the coffee table, out of the Ivory Tower of academia, and into the hands of people who cannot only use but benefit from the many insights and wisdom found from doctoral research results and findings. The goal is to continue to bridge the gap from the halls of academia into the halls of the business world. *The Refractive Thinker®* series continues to offer a resource from the many contributing doctoral scholars as they offer their chapter summaries of doctoral research well beyond the boundaries of a traditional textbook. Instead, the goal for this series is to use refractive thinking strategies to push the boundaries beyond conventional wisdom and to explore the paths not yet traveled particularly in this evolving digital age.

As we move beyond the Summer of 2019, this peer-reviewed publication offers readers insights and solutions to various challenges in working with multiple cultures. Our hope is for you to find answers regarding these unique challenges managers and leaders face in finding effective strategies to help guide your efforts in the workplace. Within these pages, scholars offer insights in access to capital for entrepreneurs to the effect of organizational vision, to include elements of the good organizational citizen, ensuring prosperous knowledge flow, escaping the refractive prism, engaging a mosaic workforce, cross-cultural competencies, the culture of retaining new teachers, and exploring a leader's DNA that impacts color, concluding with why professional educators cannot talk about the elephant in the room. Let these scholars help you find more effective ways forward.

This volume will continue to shape the conversation of future success in business to examine proven strategies for continued excellence and profitability that have come from the research and pens of professional academicians and scholars around the world. The premise is to think not only *outside the box,* but also *beyond the box,* to create new solutions, to ask new questions, to proceed forward on new roads not yet explored or traveled. Our premise is to review academic research in a simple to digest executive summary format to offer new ways for business leaders to think about effective practices for strategies in their business based on what new research has to offer specifically growing the future of business.

With this volume, we continue to include a section to the series where Dr. Cheryl Lentz, *The Academic Entrepreneur* concludes each chapter from a business point of view to link this doctoral research to applications for your business.

Remember, not only does *The Refractive Thinker®* series offer a physical book, we offer eBooks (Kindle, Nook, and Adobe eReader), and eChapters (individual chapters by author) that highlight the writings of your favorite Refractive Thinker® scholars, available through our website: www.RefractiveThinker.com, as well as www.Amazon.com . Be sure to also visit our social media to include our Facebook page, Twitter, our YouTube Channel, and our profile and groups on LinkedIN® for further discussions regarding the many ideas presented here.

We look forward to your continued support and interest of the more than 160 scholars within *the Refractive Thinker®* doctoral community who contributed to this multi award winning anthology series from around the globe. Our mission that began with Volume 1 many years ago is to bring research out of academia for application in the world of business to provide answers to the many questions asked.

Acknowledgments

The foundation of scholarly research embraces the art of asking questions—to validate and affirm, what we do, and why. Through asking the right questions, the right answers are found. Leaders often challenge the status quo, to offer alternatives and new directions, to dare to try something bold and audacious, to try something that has never been tried before. This 17th volume (19 in the series—we published Vol II three times!) of our beloved 20-time award winning *Refractive Thinker*® series required the continued belief in this new publishing model, of a peer-reviewed doctoral anthology, by those willing to continue forward on this voyage.

We are grateful for the help of many who made this collaboration possible. First, let me offer a special thank you to our **Peer Review Board**, to include Dr. Joseph Gioia, Dr. Ron Jones, and myself; and our **Board of Advisors**, to include Brian Jud and Dr. Jody Sandwisch; and media consultant / partner, Rebecca Hall-Gruyter and her amazing team.

My gratitude extends with a well-deserved thank you to our production team: Gary Rosenberg (production specialist) and Joey Root, designer of the original Refractive Thinker® logo.

Thank you. We appreciate everyone's contributions to this scholarly collaboration.

Job well done!

My best to our continued success!

Dr. Cheryl Lentz
Managing Editor and Chief Refractive Thinker®

Access to Capital for Entrepreneurs: Perspectives of Angel Investors, Venture Capitalists, and Bankers

Dr. James D. Bennett & Dr. Thomas E. Bennett, Jr.

The contribution of entrepreneurs and their newly founded firms to economic growth is difficult to overstate. Through their innovations and entrepreneurial venturing, entrepreneurs drive much of the economic activity, job creation, and cash flows that change and grow the aggregate society (Smith & Chimucheka, 2014). To finance their endeavors, entrepreneurs rely on a mix of debt and equity financing. However, entrepreneurs often struggle to obtain access to capital from outside investors and banking institutions, especially during the initial startup stage and early growth stages of their ventures (Cumming, Deloof, Manigart, & Wright, 2019; Gompers & Lerner, 2001). Thus, much may be gained by understanding better the variety of financing options available to entrepreneurs as part of the financing culture. In this chapter of *The Refractive Thinker*®, we explore the phenomenon of how entrepreneurs navigate the financing culture to obtain access to funding by utilizing their social capital and by gaining a better understanding of the different risk perspectives of outside investors and bankers.

Much has been written on the topic of entrepreneurial financing. Previous scholarly literature on entrepreneurial finance enumerates various sources and types of funding, such as venture capitalists (VCs), corporate venture capitalists, government venture capital, private equity funds, business angels (BAs), also referred to as angel investors, business angel networks, crowdfunding, bank finance, family offices, and business accelerators or incubators (Block, Colombo, Cumming, & Vismara, 2017). For this qualitative study, researchers chose to focus only on entrepreneurs, BAs, VCs, and bankers who primarily focus on industries other than the technology industry. Our exploration of this topic followed the primary research question: Does an entrepreneur's utilization of social capital and knowledge of the entrepreneurial funding culture increase their access to capital and chances of securing funding?

This organization of this article is as follows: We first introduce the topics (a) entrepreneurial finance and (b) social capital. A brief review of the relevant literature follows the introduction. Discussed in the literature review are three broad investor types and equity capital sources (a) banks, (b) BAs, and (c) VCs, as well as the topic of social capital. An in-depth overview of the literature regarding the entrepreneurial financing landscape is beyond the scope of this chapter. However, we recommend the recent literature reviews by (a) Drover et al. (2017), (b) Landström and Sørheim (2019), and (c) Wallmeroth, Wirtz, and Groh (2018), to gain an in-depth understanding of the past and present research developments related to entrepreneurial finance, as well as Cumming et al. (2019) for an in-depth view of new research directions. A description of the research process follows the literature review. A presentation of the research findings, a discussion of the implications, and suggestions for future research conclude this chapter.

Literature Review

During the startup and growth stages of an entrepreneurial endeavor, finding potential investors and access to capital are two of the entrepreneur's highest priorities. Banks, BAs, and VCs are among the most commonly known and researched sources of funding in the financing culture. According to the pecking order theory of capital structure, firm managers follow a preferred order when choosing how to finance their firm's operations (Myers & Majluf, 1984). Underlying the pecking order theory is the assumption that the expense of equity financing increases in proportion to the information asymmetries between the firm and the potential investors. Myers and Majluf (1984) explained that firms (a) prefer to finance their operations with retained earnings over debt and equity financing, (b) prefer short-term debt financing over long-term debt financing, and (c) prefer debt financing over equity financing. Since the 1980s, scholarly research related to startup investment decision-making types increased.

In their seminal article, Cosh, Cumming, and Hughes (2009) examined the selection criteria that outside investors use to make investment decisions on entrepreneurial ventures. Specifically, Cosh et al. explained that although entrepreneurs' desire external financing and often obtain external financing, frequently entrepreneurs do not obtain their most preferred type of external financing. Moreover, Cosh et al. found that small firms frequently obtained their financing from private individuals or Bas, while VCs preferred fast growing, younger firms. Even so, Cosh et al. emphasized that not many fast growing, young firms obtain VC funding because of the high rejection rate.

Banks

Banks provide startup, growth, and operational capital to entrepreneurs in the form of debt financing, called loans. For most companies, the main financing source is debt (Hirsch & Walz, 2019). One banker interviewed explained,

> In our American society, banks play the role of a financial steward in that banks must safely facilitate the transfer of wealth, earned and owned by older generation, to finance the dreams and ambitions of a younger generation for the price of interest.

To be a good financial steward, banks must limit risks associated with lending money to hopeful borrowers. Banks do so by making loans that conform to U.S. federal and state regulations, as well as to internal lending policies. For example, to qualify for a loan, banks require borrowers (a) to provide evidence of their historical, current, and projected cash flows and (b) to provide collateral as a security to ensure the repayment of the loan. However, not all hopeful borrowers qualify for the loans they desire.

Hechavarría, Matthews, and Reynolds (2015) explained that debt investors use things like covenants and collateral to mitigate the risks of lending money by ensuring that borrowers have some *skin in the game*. Hechavarría et al. emphasized that having skin in the game motivates borrowers to generate revenues enough to cover their debt payments. However, failure from underinvestment can result when borrowers focus too much on debt repayment and not enough on value creation (Hechavarría et al., 2015). If entrepreneurs run out of money or do not qualify for a loan, they often turn to alternative sources of capital, such as BAs and VCs.

Angel Investors

BAs provide the majority of private equity seed capital to startup ventures in the United States. According to the Angel Capital Association (ACA) (2017b), "Angel investors provide $25B to 70,000 companies annually—90% of outside equity for startups—but very little is known about angels themselves" (para. 1). The ACA (2017a) surveyed 1,959 angel investors and found that (a) 54.8% of BAs had previously founded or been the chief executive officer (CEO) of their own startups, (b) the average angel investment size was $25,000, and (c) on average, BAs invest in 7–11 investments at the same time. Additionally, the ACA (2017a) reported that BAs find their prospective investments 89.3% via angel groups, 51.8% through friends, and 58.0% via direct contact with the entrepreneurs. The ACA (2017a) found that entrepreneurial-minded BAs invested larger amounts, invested in more companies, got a higher return on investment (ROI), and took more active roles within their invested-in companies.

BAs tend to have similar ages, similar professional experiences, similar investment preferences, and similar financial backgrounds. Wong, Bhatia, and Freeman (2009) differentiated between official BAs or *accredited investors* and unofficial BAs and estimated that BAs accounted for 23% of the BA total population. As defined by the United Sates Securities and Exchange Commission (SEC) Rule 501 of Regulation D, an accredited investor is (a) an individual whose income is $200,000, or whose joint income is $300,000, in the two most recent years, (b) with an expectation of meeting that income again, or (c) by an individual with individual or joint net wealth of $1million, not including their primary residence. Despite the many personal similarities of BAs, angel investments do not follow a typical processes or terms.

Venture Capitalists

VCs are professional investors who raise funds from other individuals, companies, and pension funds to invest in startup or early stage growth companies. VC investments carry a high risk because VCs typically invest in pre-profit companies. However, VC investments are less risky than BA investments because VCs tend to follow more sophisticated investment decision criteria and processes than BAs (Drover et al., 2017). According to the PitchBook National Venture Capital Association (NVCA) (2019), VC investment in the United States reached a record high $130.9 billion in 2018. PitchBook-NVCA also reported an increase in the deal sizes and valuations and a decrease in the overall number of VC deals. For example, 12.8% of the VC deals in the United States obtained more than $25 million in funding.

The Different Risk Perspectives Within the Financing Culture

How people perceive the risk in a particular investment affects whether they decide to make the investment at all, and, if they do make the investment, what kind of return they expect for the presumed amount of risk involved. Risk is the possibility of suffering harm or loss, danger. Entrepreneurs, investors, and bankers represent a continuum of perspectives about risk as it applies to their investment of money in a business venture (see Table 1).

TABLE 1. *PERSPECTIVES OF RISK WITHIN THE FINANCING CULTURE*

	Entrepreneur	Angel Investor	Banker
Risk Position	100% Risk—All in	Risk limited to amount of investment	Trying to eliminate or reduce risk to .25% of all loans
Reward Opportunity	Maximum wealth creation. Compensation for job.	Maximizing return on investment	Fixed interest rate, currently in the range of 5–7%
Focus	How do I make this a successful company maximizing wealth creation for my family, and make a difference in the world?	How do I maximize the return on my investment in a business I understand with people I believe in?	How do I minimize the risk of loss in my investment and maximize the possibility that my loan will be repaid?

The Entrepreneur's Perspective

Entrepreneurs represent the highest risk tolerance in the financing culture. This is because entrepreneurs risk their reputation, career, financial resources, and time with family to make their companies successful. As one entrepreneur interviewed noted, "When I began my company, it was a tough decision because I knew I had the most to gain and the most to lose if my business venture didn't work out." Another entrepreneur interviewed emphasized,

> The difference between a dreamer and an entrepreneur is the entrepreneur goes beyond his or her dreams and takes the risk of investing all they have and all they can raise or borrow from others, to make their own dreams come true.

New ideas of companies are inherently riskier than long established ones.

In some startups, 100% of the funding comes from equity as opposed to debt. This is so because most new companies (a) lack valuable collateral to secure the debt and (b) lose money in their early years, which means they cannot demonstrate to a bank their ability to repay debt. Consequently, entrepreneurs rely on equity investments from alternative sources to sustain and grow their business.

Once a business is recognized as established, bank loans are easier to get. That recognition only happens after the startup begins to own assets of value and achieves profitability enough to debt service the loan. Typically, borrowers with a debt service coverage ratio (DSCR) of 1.2x conform to a bank's loan policy and show enough profitability to comfortably debt service their loan. However, on a case by case basis, banks can waive DSCR requirements when it makes sense for borrowers whose DSCR is less than 1.2x.

Once companies become profitable, they often fund much of their growth with debt from banks. As one entrepreneur noted,

> My favorite partners are banks, because banks will put up most of the money I need despite their limited rate of return. When I'm already committing 100% of my time, energy, and life to my business, it doesn't seem like a big leap to also personally guarantee 100% of the debt of my company.

In other words, entrepreneurs expect that they will need to make sacrifices to secure the initial financing for their ventures, even if that means risking everything they own.

The Angel Investor's Perspective

BAs represent the next highest risk tolerance within the financing culture but less risk than the entrepreneurs. The limit of a BAs risk is the amount of their investment. As a result, BAs accept more risk than banks because BA investments are normally unsecured, and the expectation of repayment is sometime in the future. One BA interviewed explained, "I never put more than 5% of my net worth into one deal. That way I can limit my risk." Another BA interviewed said,

> Generally, my expected rate of return is related to the amount of risk in the business undertaking. On long established industries that are highly regulated like a banks or utilities, I expect a lower return than on new industries with less structure and more risk.

Consequently, to obtain BA financing, entrepreneurs must present an investment opportunity that makes it easy for a BA to perceive that their investment risks are worth their anticipated or projected rewards.

Many BAs mitigate the risks associated with their investments by investing in multiple deals at once and by keeping a laser focus on their investment objectives. The BA investment objective is three-fold: (a) identify prospect businesses within industries they understand, (b) determine the believability of the founding entrepreneurs, and (c) focus on maximizing the ROI in a reasonable amount of time. Normally, BAs have a 5–7-year exit strategy that concludes with a liquidity event, such as an initial public offering (IPO) or the sale off the company. On the other hand, some BAs prefer to get their original investment back quickly, but, after recouping their original investment, prefer to let their remaining interest in the company grow into the future. Another smaller group of BAs prefer to be long-term equity investors from the start. Consequently, entrepreneurs need to make sure to align their own interests with their investors' interests regarding future liquidity in the stock.

The Banker's Perspective

Bankers represent the lowest risk tolerance within the financing culture. As an industry, banks have historically kept a reserve for possible loan losses of 1.0% and have limited the actual net loan losses to less than 0.25% (Board of Governors of the Federal Reserve System [BGFRS], 2019). In general, banks make money by managing the net interest margin between their yield on earning assets, which are mostly loans, and their cost of funds, which are mostly deposits, to about 4.0%. Additionally, banks manage their cost of doing business, which includes net loan losses but excludes interest expense, to 3.0% of their assets. Successful banks earn a 1.0% return on their assets managed. Banks focus on how they can minimize the risk of losses on their loans. A banker interviewed explained,

> Bankers take less risk because they invest other people's money. Bankers have a fiduciary duty to repay their depositors, whose money they are investing in loans. Essentially, a bank's purpose is to manage the risk in the transfer of wealth in the community, between an older generation of depositors and a younger generation of borrowers. Thus, banks have a duty to be conservative.

Consequently, banks have a very low tolerance for risk of possible losses.

On the other hand, bankers have the lowest profitability in a business deal; a fixed interest rate on their loan. A key difference between bankers and investors is that most bankers have never been entrepreneurs. While some bankers may invest in the stock market or in small real estate projects, most have never had to risk everything to grow a business. As a result, the prospect of a total loss scares them.

Bankers limit their risk exposure by requiring borrowers (a) to pledge collateral with a market value in excess of the loan and (b) to contractually guarantee the repayment of the loan. Additionally, bankers make loan agreements with borrowers to create structure in the deal that limits the risk to the bank and maximizes the profitability that the loan will be repaid. One banker we interviewed emphasized,

> Bankers want their loan risks to be as boring as possible, which means that bankers want their risk position to be behind the risk position of the entrepreneur and the investors. That way, if something goes wrong, the threat of losing their investment motivates the entrepreneurs and investors to solve the problem and repay the loan.

Thus, the size of risk and not the size of profit is the primary motivator for bankers.

How to Raise Equity Capital and Borrow Money

Entrepreneurs access to equity capital and borrow money based on their needs and on their company's position in the business life cycle. During the startup phase, most of an entrepreneur's initial financial capital is from personal savings or from close family and friends (see Appendix A). During the business growth, expansion, and acquisition stages, entrepreneurs' transition to financial capital from BAs, VCs, banks, and occasionally suppliers (see Appendix A). Finally, entrepreneurs of mature business often experience the exit of BAs and VCs and increase their reliance on bank debt and supplier financing (see Appendix A).

Sources of Equity Capital

An entrepreneur's first source of equity capital normally comes from their personal financial resources. A personal financial investment as well as an investment of sweat equity allow the entrepreneur to have skin in the game, which is often a prerequisite to attract investment from others. An entrepreneur's financial resources may include (a) cash, (b) savings, or (c) asset-to-cash conversions, such as a home equity line of credit. Entrepreneurs who give stock options or profit-sharing opportunities to key employees and managers create an opportunity for those employees and managers to also have skin in the game. Entrepreneurs increase their employee's long-term commitment and loyalty to the company by giving key personnel and managers opportunities to own stock, earn stock options, and participate in profit-sharing (Chang, Fu, Low, & Zhang, 2015). Put differently, when everyone important to the company has skin in the game, the financial outcomes of the entrepreneur, managers, and employees align with the financial outcomes of any outside investors so that the failure or success of the company is shared by all.

An entrepreneur's second primary source for equity capital is usually investment from his or her family, close friends, and business partners (see Appendix B). According to Glaeser, Laibson, and Sacerdote's (2002) definition, an individual's social capital is comprised of "a person's social characteristics—including social skills, charisma, and the size of his Rolodex—which enables him to reap market and non-market returns from interactions with others" (p. F438). An entrepreneur's social capital includes friends, family, communities of origin and profession, religious and academic communities, and other networked people and people groups.

For friends and family, the decision to invest in the entrepreneurial venture may rely more on their fundamental trust in the entrepreneur than on their depth of understanding for the entrepreneur's business plans. An entrepreneur interviewed whose company grossed over $10.2 billion in sales in 2018 noted that the initial equity capital for the venture came from a getting personal bank loan, from his partner borrowing money from a family member, and from three of his friends investing in the venture. He understood that an important reason why people invested and made he and his partner loans was his reputation for successfully starting previous ventures. In fact, he emphasized that because the business the concept for the business he started was a new, not everyone understood how his business would succeed. Ultimately, his entrepreneurial venture lost money for the first 3 years before it became a huge success.

For entrepreneurs who need to raise more a lot of money, using their social capital to expand their personal network is very important (see Appendix B). Among the entrepreneurs interviewed, one who raised over $150 million for his own ventures said he expanded his personal fundraising network by developing a tree of investor relationships. He explained that entrepreneurs should start with a list of 20 people who know they well; hoping that 5–6 will say yes. Then, entrepreneurs should ask those 5–6 investors for names of 10–20 more prospects each and call on those people; hoping that 20 or so of those 50–100 will say yes. Then, again, entrepreneurs should ask those investors for referrals and so on. He emphasized, however, that entrepreneurs must be ready for many prospect investors to say no.

Further, he advised that for entrepreneurs who plan to have more than 25 investors, they need to hire an attorney to prepare a Private Placement Memorandum (PPM). In the PPM, the entrepreneur lays out their business proposal to investors, including planned management and directors and a description of all the possible risks associated with the investment. The purpose of the PPM is to help the entrepreneur avoid potential liability if the deal does not work out by providing all the relevant details of the venture.

Social Capital Impacts Access to Financial Capital

Developing a personal network of trusting relationships, also called social capital, is a key success factor in accessing financial capital (see Appendix B). Many members of marginalized communities lack knowledge about how to access capital, especially bank debt. The impact of social capital and intellectual capital was an issue raised by minority businesspeople during the interviews. One interviewee observed that people who grow up in poor homes learn how to spend the scarce money available to them but rarely learn how to save money and invest it in things that make money. Another interviewee said,

People in marginalized communities have been traumatized. They often survive paycheck-to-paycheck without enough money to meet family emergencies. So, when they start out, entrepreneurs from marginalized communities often don't understand the importance of credit reports or even how a credit report impacts their access to capital. For example, when an emergency like a health problem or accident happens, they get emotional and do something stupid that negatively impacts their whole lives, including access to capital.

Minority businesspeople also noted that much of their community lacks the intellectual capital or a basic education about financial management and how to access capital. In minority communities, access to capital often comes from individuals with money who make personal loans or investments in people's businesses at very high interest rates. In these cases, the lender or investor relies on personal information about the entrepreneur's reputation and the reputation of the entrepreneur's family instead of on a credit report. This personal information may come from interviews with a pastor, parent, or grandparent who vouches for the character of the businessperson and promises to help the individual make payments if he or she falls behind.

Some community entrepreneurs noted that a primary reason for their success were lessons learned during their childhood and mentorship from their parents. One entrepreneur noted,

> My parents taught me to work hard, save money, and invest in income-producing assets. By the time I was 15, I had saved up enough money from mowing lawns to make a down payment on my first commercial real estate property. My dad co-signed my first loan. Also, early on in my career I partnered with a very successful older businessman in my industry and learned from him how to make good deals.

Another entrepreneur who was an immigrant from India noted,

> In the Indian and Asian communities there is a high emphasis on education, including college degrees. Most young people of Indian descent will graduate from college with no student loan debt. We feel it is a sacred duty to educate our children.

Another entrepreneur who was an immigrant from Vietnam said,

> Social capital, which covers a wide range of background, affiliation, and relationships plays a profound role in access to financial capital. In my case, I became known to investors and bankers through my academic and professional networks. I benefited both from members of my cultural and religious communities, as well as from members of communities I was invited to join after proving my work ethic, integrity, and sincerity. The communities I was involved in helped me with management advise and references to other businesses for supplies and sales.

Being a part of more than one social network was critical to success of my entrepreneurial ventures.

In these scenarios, some cultural groups never learned how to save, invest, create business loans, and borrow money. As a result, those communities struggled to gain access to financial capital. On the other hand, those who learned about financial management early in life or through school and had a good mentor knew how to navigate use their social capital to gain access to financial capital.

Conclusion

Entrepreneurs and their firms drive much of the aggregate society's economic activity and growth. To finance their endeavors, entrepreneurs rely on a mix of debt and equity financing. However, entrepreneurs often struggle to obtain access to capital from outside investors and banking institutions, especially during the initial startup stage and early growth stages of their ventures (Cumming, Deloof, Manigart, & Wright, 2019; Gompers & Lerner, 2001). We explored in this article the phenomenon of how entrepreneurs navigate the financing culture to obtain access to funding by utilizing their social capital and by gaining a better understanding of the different risk perspectives of outside investors and bankers.

Thus, much may be gained by understanding better the variety of financing options available to entrepreneurs as part of the financing culture. Results indicated that BAs, VCs, and bankers primarily look at the character and integrity of the entrepreneur and the perceived risk of the venture to make their investment decision. Also, we found that BAs, VCs, and bankers differ in how they perceive the risks of a venture as well as what they expect as a return for their investment. Entrepreneurs can increase their chances of accessing capital for their ventures by (a) utilizing their social capital to find interested investors and (b) by clearly conveying their integrity and readiness in their fundraising pitches to BAs, VCs, and banks. Last, to increase their chances at securing funding, entrepreneurs must show BAs, VCs, and banks that their risk and reward for an investment in the venture is reasonable.

REFERENCES

Angel Capital Association. (2017a). *The American angel.* Retrieved from https://www.theamericanangel.org/

Angel Capital Association. (2017b). *Who is the American angel?* Retrieved from https://docs.wixstatic.com/ugd/ecd9be_aa3c0cd8a09e4116a3f88967a5232949.pdf

Block, J. H., Colombo, M. G., Cumming, D. J., & Vismara, S. (2017). New players in entrepreneurial finance and why they are there. *Small Business Economics, 50,* 239–250. doi:10.1007/s11187–016–9826–6

Board of Governors of the Federal Reserve System. (2019). Charge-off and delinquency rates on loans and leases at commercial banks. Retrieved from https://www.federalreserve.gov/releases/chargeoff/chgallsa.htm

Chang, X., Fu, K., Low, A., & Zhang, W. (2015). Non-executive employee stock options and corporate innovation. *Journal of Financial Economics, 115,* 168–188. doi:10.1016/j.jfineco.2014.09.002

Cosh, A., Cumming, D., & Hughes, A. (2009). Outside entrepreneurial capital. *The Economic Journal, 119,* 1494–1533. doi:10.1111/j.1468–0297.2009.02270.x

Cumming, D., Deloof, M., Manigart, S., & Wright, M. (2019). New directions in entrepreneurial finance. *Journal of Banking & Finance, 100,* 252–260. doi:10.1016/j.jbankfin.2019.02.008

Drover, W., Busenitz, L., Matusik, S., Townsend, D., Anglin, A., & Dushnitsky, G. (2017). A review and road map of entrepreneurial equity financing research: Venture capital, corporate venture capital, angel investment, crowdfunding, and accelerators. *Journal of Management, 43,* 1820–1853. doi:10.1177/0149206317690584

Glaeser, E. L., Laibson, D., & Sacerdote, B. (2002). An economic approach to social capital*. *The Economic Journal, 112*(483), F437–F458. doi:10.1111/1468–0297.00078

Gompers, P., & Lerner, J. (2001). The venture capital revolution. *Journal of Economic Perspectives, 15,* 145–168. doi:10.1257/jep.15.2.145

Hechavarría, D. M., Matthews, C. H., & Reynolds, P. D. (2015). Does start-up financing influence start-up speed? Evidence from the panel study of entrepreneurial dynamics. *Small Business Economics, 46,* 137–167. doi:10.1007/s11187–015–9680-y

Hirsch, J., & Walz, U. (2019). The financing dynamics of newly founded firms. *Journal of Banking & Finance, 100,* 261–272. doi:10.1016/j.jbankfin.2018.11.009

Landström, H., & Sørheim, R. (2019). The ivory tower of business angel research. *Venture Capital, 21,* 97–119. doi:10.1080/13691066.2019.1559879

Myers, S. C., & Majluf, N. S. (1984). Corporate financing and investment decisions when firms have information that investors do not have. *Journal of Financial Economics, 13,* 187–221. doi:10.1016/0304–405x(84)90023–0

PitchBook National Venture Capital Association. (2019). *Venture monitor: 1Q 2019.* Retrieved from https://pitchbook.com/news/reports/4q-2018-pitchbook-nvca-venture-monitor

Smith, W., & Chimucheka, T. (2014). Entrepreneurship, economic growth and entrepreneurship theories. *Mediterranean Journal of Social Sciences, 5,* 160–168. doi:10.5901/mjss.2014.v5n14p160

U.S. Securities and Exchange Commission (SEC). (2019). *Title 17: Commodity and Securities Exchanges Part 230: General Rules and Regulations, Securities Act of 1933 §230.501: Definitions and terms used in Regulation D.* Retrieved from https://www.ecfr.gov/cgi-bin/retrieveECFR?gp=&SID=8edfd12967d69c-024485029d968ee737&r=SECTION&n=7y3.0.1.1.12.0.46.176

Wallmeroth, J., Wirtz, P., & Groh, A. P. (2018). Venture capital, angel financing, and crowdfunding of entrepreneurial ventures: A literature review. *Foundations and Trends® in Entrepreneurship, 14*(1), 1–129. doi:10.1561/0300000066

Wong, A., Bhatia, M., & Freeman, Z. (2009). Angel finance: The other venture capital. *Strategic Change, 18,* 221–230. doi:10.1002/jsc.849

APPENDIX A. *Access to Financial Capital at Various Stages of Need*

	Entrepreneur's personal capital	Family and close friends' capital	Angel investor capital
Start-up business phase	Most start their business with their financial capital and that of family and close friends. This covers start-up costs, early operating losses, and other costs not associated with asset acquisition like marketing, fees, licenses.		Angel investors may expand the start-up funding.
Acquisition of assets phase	Some cash may be used for equity in either fixed assets (RE/equipment) or accounts receivable and inventory.		Angel investors may expand cash available to use as equity in assets
Rapid growth in initial market	Equity invested by the entrepreneur, family, friends, and angel investors is usually needed to pay for rapidly increasing account receivables, hiring new staff, paying for technology and marketing expenses. If additional equity is raised from investors, it may be useful to find investors who will use the product or service and/or who are influential in the market being served.		
Expansion into new markets	If it is necessary to raise equity capital to fund expansion into new markets, it may be helpful to raise all or part of the money from people in the new market to help the company develop local social capital.		
Stabilizing into a mature company	Entrepreneurs, family, and angel investors normally want to start receiving cash flow from their investments as the company matures. This can be accomplished by dividends, stock repurchases, going public or the sale of the company.		

Venture capital	Bank debt	Suppliers/leases
NA	Banks may make personal loans to entrepreneurs, family and friends to convert assets to cash to invest in a new business venture. It is difficult without a strong guarantor for banks to do much start-up financing directly to a business.	
NA	Banks may finance purchase of real estate and equipment. With the backing of SBA or USDA or a strong guarantor, banks may provide financing for working capital.	Landlords may lease facilities. Equipment cos. may lease equipment. Suppliers may provide long-term credit for inventory.
May qualify for venture capital investment	As a company grows and becomes profitable, it can qualify for an increasing amount of bank debt.	As a company grows and becomes profitable, suppliers may increase the availability of credit and extension of terms.
If a company has proven success in an initial market, it may qualify for venture capital funding for rapid expansion into new markets.	If the company is earning enough income in initial markets to service additional debt, banks may finance expansion into new markets, particularly with a strong guarantor.	Suppliers, leasers, and landlords may also be sources of funding for expansion into new markets. They may want a bank letter of credit to support the expanded venture.
BAs and VCs have a 5–7-year window on their investment and expect to be paid off by a liquidity event in the company.	As companies stabilize and become profitable, bank debt is often used for working capital, purchasing facilities, and buying out early investors.	Suppliers normally are willing to improve credit terms as companies become mature and increasingly profitable.

APPENDIX B. *ACCESS TO FINANCIAL CAPITAL IMPACTED BY SOCIAL CAPITAL AND INTELLECTUAL*

	Increased availability	Decreased availability
Social capital Networks of relationships that entrepreneurs and their associates have that may be called on to help get something accomplished.	Being part of racial, ethnic, or national origin groups where relationships are mutually supportive increases access to capital.	Being part of racial, ethnic or national origin groups where relationships are not mutually supportive reduces access to capital.
	Being part of academic, social, or professional organizations where relationships are mutually supportive increases access to capital.	Not being part of academic, social, professional organizations where relationships are mutually supportive reduces access to capital.
	Having a mentor who coaches you on how to save, invest, borrow, and raise capital increases access to capital.	Not having a mentor who coaches you on how to save, invest, borrow reduces your access to capital.
	Being part of a minority group where federal, state, or tribal programs exist to help entrepreneurs increase access to capital.	Not being part of a minority group where programs exist to help provide access to capital reduces access to capital.
Intellectual capital The knowledge an individual or group of individuals possess that may be used to produce wealth, multiply assets, increase competitive advantage and/or enhance the value of their other forms of capital.	Being raised in a family where saving and investing in income-producing assets increases knowledge about how to gain access to capital.	Not being raised in a family where saving and investing in income-producing assets reduces access to capital.
	Successfully completing academic or training programs on how to save, invest, borrow, and raise capital increases access to capital.	Not successfully completing academic or training programs on how to save and raise equity capital reduces access to capital.
	Working for a company that either invests or lends money to entrepreneurs or for an entrepreneur who raises equity capital or borrows money increases access to capital.	Not working in a company that practices investing, lending, or borrowing reduces access to capital.

THOUGHTS FROM THE ACADEMIC ENTREPRENEUR

The problem to be solved:

- Accessing capital for entrepreneurs.

The goals:

- Understanding better the variety of financing options available to entrepreneurs as well as how an entrepreneur's social capital influences the initial funding decisions of equity investors and bankers.

The questions to ask:

- Does an entrepreneur's utilization of social capital and knowledge of the entrepreneurial funding culture increase their access to capital and chances of securing funding?

- What are some similarities and differences between outside investors and bankers that entrepreneurs should know and prepare for to increase their chances of securing financing?

- How does an entrepreneur's social capital influence the funding decisions of equity investors and bankers?

Today's Business Application:

- BAs, VCs, and bankers primarily look at the character and integrity of the entrepreneur and the perceived risk of the venture to make their investment decision.

- BAs, VCs, and bankers differ in how they perceive the risks of a venture as well as what they expect as a return for their investment.

- Entrepreneurs increase their chances of accessing capital when their fundraising pitches to BAs, VCs, and banks clearly convey their integrity, readiness, and a reasonably matched risk and reward for an investment in their venture.

- Entrepreneurs increase their chances of accessing capital when they use their social capital as a resource to identify potential investors with common interests and histories who are favorably disposed to investing in entrepreneurial ventures.

About the Authors . . .

Dr. James D. Bennett resides in Tulsa, OK. Dr. James is currently Vice President and Credit Analyst for First Oklahoma Bank (FOB). Previously, Dr. James served as Corporate Secretary and as a Commercial Lender for FOB. Dr. James has a Bachelor of Science and a Master's in English from Belmont University, as well as a Doctorate in Business Administration from Walden University.

In addition to co-founding FOB, Dr. James has over 15 years of experience serving as a business manager, entrepreneur, songwriter, publisher, and sales consultant. Dr. James has also served as a sales consultant for Hemphill, LLC., a leader in the wireless communication towers industry.

Dr. James has appeared on Fox Business Network's hit TV show *Strange Inheritance* season 2, episode 18. Also, Dr. James was the Lennon Award Winner and Grand Prize Winner in the John Lennon Songwriting Contest in 2012.

Dr. James has ghostwritten articles for national publications including *Forbes.com, ThinkAdvisor.com, HJRGlobal.com, JFSWealthAdvisors, USA Financial,* and more. Additional published works include his dissertation: *Profit Enhancement Strategies for the Spotify Music Streaming Business Model.*

To reach Dr. James D. Bennett for information on community banking, strategic planning, or guest speaking, please visit his **website:** https://www.linkedin.com/in/jamesbennett918/ or **e-mail:** DrJimiBennett@gmail.com

Dr. Thomas E. Bennett, Jr. is a 5th generation Oklahoman with over 41 years at three of Oklahoma's fastest growing banks. He is currently Chairman & Co-CEO of First Oklahoma Bank, which has grown in 9 years to over $700 million in assets. Dr. Thomas has a Bachelor's in Sociology from Oklahoma State University, a Master's in Public Administration from Harvard University, and a Ph.D. in Business Administration from OSU.

Dr. Thomas has served as a White House Fellow and Special Assistant to the Comptroller of the Currency in Washington, D.C. and Senior Advisor and Coordinator of Strategic Planning for the Oklahoma Department of Commerce. Dr. Bennett's professional has also served as State Chairman of the Robert Morris Associates, and National Director of the Independent Bankers Association. In 2018, Dr. Thomas joined the Advisory Board for Oklahoma State University's school of Global Studies and Partnerships.

Dr. Thomas has written over 70 articles in national publications including *Inc.* magazine, *The Robert Morris Journal of Commercial Bank Lending,* the Tulsa World, and The Rural News.

To reach Dr. Thomas E. Bennett, Jr. for information on community banking, strategic planning, or guest speaking, please visit his **website: https://www. firstoklahomabank.com/** or **e-mail: tom.bennett@firstoklahomabank. com**

CHAPTER 2

The Effect of the Organizational Vision on Remote Employees Engagement

Dr. Frank Musmar

According to Gallup (2017), more than 70% of U.S. employees lack engagement in their work. Adkins (2017) defined work engagement as involvement, enthusiasm, and commitment to work, and workplace. Although organizational leaders increasingly tried to increase employee engagement (Anitha, 2014), the rate at which employees become disengaged in their work continues to increase in the United States (Gallup, 2017). From 2005 to 2017, the number of U.S. remote workers increased (Tugend, 2018). With the rapid growth and expansion of remote working options, organizational leaders became concerned about their ability to build, manage, and maintain an engaged workplace with employees who will never physically be in the office space (Adkins, 2015). Organizational vision experts suggested implementing the organizational vision to create an engagement culture (Piaget, 2013), a work environment where the leaders create a culture defined by mission, values, beliefs, principles, and employee engagement (Roark, 2013). In this chapter of the Refractive Thinker®, I present an overview of the effect of the organizational vision on maintaining, strengthening, or eroding the remote workplace engagement.

Background of the Study

Researchers focused on traditional factors that influence engagement and the relationship between engagement and organizational vision (Adkins, 2017). Kahn (1990) defined engagement as employing and expressing selves physically, cognitively, and emotionally during role performances. Kahn provided the foundational context for understanding how theories of motivation influence employee engagement (as cited in Hackbarth, 2017). Current literature on employee engagement borrowed from Kahn failed to address the emerging phenomenon of remote workplace engagement (as cited in De Menezes & Kelliher, 2016). In early 2017, Gallup researchers surveyed thousands of employees globally to collect data on the engagement levels of remote workers. Engagement increases when employees spend some time working remotely and some time working in a traditional office (Mann & Adkins, 2017). Employees who experience this blended working arrangement have higher levels of engagement than those employees who do not (Mann & Adkins, 2017). Effective leaders, who understand the remote work environment can increase productivity and profitability, promote organizational commitment, which leads to organizational growth.

The research on remote employee engagement is minimal and open for discovery outside of that traditional framework (Mann & Harter, 2016). The Musmar (2019) study added to the knowledge of the workplace engagement experiences of remote workers. The results provided organizational leaders with the tools and information needed to better understand how to manage the engagement levels of their remote workers (Musmar, 2019). The purpose of the Musmar study was to explore the effect of the organizational vision on maintaining, strengthening, or eroding the workplace engagement of 20 remote faculties in the United States who worked in remote educational climate for a minimum of 2 years to improve productivity and promote organizational growth.

Measuring Levels of Employee Engagement

Organizational leaders focus on measuring engagement quantitatively using annual surveys instead of improving it, resulting in a worldwide engagement crisis (Mann & Harter, 2016). If leaders and stakeholders of organizations base their employee engagement climate on an annual quantitative survey, then an opportunity is missed to positively impact their cultures of engagement (Fuller, 2014). Engagement is dynamic and requires continuous addressing at varying points as it emerges and not only at predetermined annual points in time (Fuller, 2014). Understanding how remote workers experience workplace engagement is, and managers who supervise remote workers is vital to define engagement (Aon Hewitt, 2015).

The engaged employees work with commitment and passion and feel a profound connection to their organization (Adkins, 2016). Engaged employees work to drive innovation and move the organization forward (Reilly, 2014). The best concepts of engaged employees describe the dynamic nature of employee engagement versus the other factors that attributed to engagement (Crawford, Rich, Buckman, & Bergeron, 2014). Musmar (2019) provides the organizational leaders with the tools and information needed to better understand how to manage the engagement levels of their remote workers.

Varying interpretations of organizational engagement can lead to an in-depth analysis of the engagement that exists within the organizational context (Turker & Altuntas, 2015). The cultures of engagement provide employees an opportunity to contribute to the vision of the organization utilizing their skills and provide opportunities to engage in workplace flexibilities that enhance their work-life balance (Alvesson & Sveningsson, 2015). Creating this type of engagement is something organizational leaders must do deliberately and is not something accomplished by happenstance (Parris, 2015).

The Organizational Vision

Organizational vision is an effective leadership strategy for any organization to stay competitive and thrive (McGregor & Doshi, 2015). The organizational vision is a comprehensive description and a clear guide to what an organization would like to accomplish and be successful in the future (Traphagan, 2015). The vision is a simple statement of purpose that emphasizes simplicity, innovation, and dedication. Clarity, challenge, stability, and the ability to inspire are compelling components of visions that make a significant impact on employee engagement (Smith & Garcia, 2016). Leaders that use vision as an effective leadership strategy can increase organizational productivity and performance.

Employees and managers assist in the overall composition of the organization's vision because they are whom the organization uses to identify itself (Alvesson & Sveningsson, 2015). Ultimately, the managers must keep the corporate vision alive through their actions and behaviors (McGregor & Doshi, 2015). The idea of organizational vision should be well defined and understood by management, leadership, scholars, and practitioners. Employees express a higher level of commitment to an organization and lower attrition rates when the organization's top leadership and employees exhibit the same attributes of the entire organization (Nickson, 2016). Authentic leaders who promoted and supported flexible-orientated organizational vision led to higher employee engagement (Azanza et al., 2013). Management and leadership scholar-practitioners often relate increased performance levels within an organization to a strong organizational vision amongst the organization's employees, which lead to an increase in organizational productivity and performance.

A positive correlation exists between organizational leaders developing strong positive relationships and developing and maintaining visions of engagement; these relationships provide the needed foundation to build and sustain active engagement (O'Brien, 2014). The outcomes of these positive relationships are beneficial for the employer and employees. The employer often benefits from having a more productive, present, satisfied, and engaged employee; the employee often benefits from receiving additional benefits such as a preferred work schedule and overtime (Colletta, Hoffman, Stone, & Bennett, 2016). The emerging remote working environment challenges the preset notions and understandings organizational leaders have about how to increase and sustain engagement, which makes understanding organization-person fit a critical factor in examining what vision engage diverse types of workers (Peh & Wee, 2015).

Remote Work Culture

Research remains limited in terms of defining the emerging of the remote work organizational culture and the engagement level of such culture (Adkins, 2016). What remote workers perceive to be their organizational culture may significantly vary from the office culture and, more importantly, from what their managers think (Saks 2017). Remote workers most often have never stepped foot into the physical office space and, therefore, do not have a frame of reference for what the corporate environment is, let alone their manager's definition or expectation for workplace engagement (Reynolds, 2011). Organizational leaders must apply the same office frame reference on remote workers to maintain a high level of engagement among remote employees.

Organizational leaders should ensure that employees are the

right fit to function in a completely remote work environment successfully. The challenge organizational leaders' face in the modern workplace is there is no clear definition or method for identifying who would be a successful remote worker because there is neither clear definition nor measurement to a remote environment. Researchers need to identify and define the virtual organizational culture and the impact of the remote culture on individuals and organizations. Some employees struggle within the traditional working environment to fit in with the organizational culture in their offices, and now they must determine how to fit into an unidentified virtual organizational culture. Workplace isolation is one of the major detractors of remote work (Mann & Adkins, 2017). As leaders in the modern workplace struggle to identify what remote organizational culture is, there is an emerging phenomenon of remote workers has increased feelings of isolation, loneliness, and disconnection from their colleagues and office culture (Sutherland, 2015).

Visionary Leadership and Remote Workers

Each leader defines his or her vision (Al Saifi, 2015). Leaders develop a vision, rationally, and objectively, often intuitively and subjectively (Cao, Huo, Li, & Zhao, 2015). Visionary leadership varies from leader to leader on critical dimensions (Naqshbandi, Kaur, Sehgal, & Subramaniam, 2015). Leaders induce their followers to act on the vision by using a range of techniques, such as legitimate authority, modeling, intellectual stimulation, goal-setting, rewarding and punishing, organizational restructuring, and team-building (Jordan, Werner, & Venter, 2015). In the traditional workplace, leaders can physically observe the actions and interactions of their employees and adjust their work and management approach based on their direct observations. When there are changes, leaders address the changed behaviors of their employees, implementing an intervention, or altering the organizational vision (Pinho, Ana, & Dibb, 2014).

Leaders who desire to fix their employees' behaviors show the critical nature organizational vision possesses within an organization, and the way vision is a driving force in sustaining and normalizing the working environment (Nor, Shamsuddin, & Wahab, 2015). When leaders try to implement change in an environment that does not support change, the implementation will more than likely fail. If there is a corporate vision that supports change, then leaders will have a better opportunity to positively impact performance in that work environment (Benn, Dunphy, & Griffiths, 2014). Developing a vision of change is critical in sustaining the change events the leaders implement.

During employment orientation programs, organizational leaders can impart their espoused values and beliefs with new employees to ensure the organization vision definition at the onset of employment (Klien, Polin, & Leigh Sutton, 2015). During this period, leaders can also share with their new employees the salient and tangible aspects of that vision in practice (Solomon, 2014). Employee socialization programs also assist leaders in visually identifying and getting to know employees, so they are better able to communicate with them in informal ways such as when they meet in hallways, elevators, and informal meetings (Solomon, 2014).

Finding the preferred corporate vision reaching remote workers is a challenge for the organizational leaders without the standard practices that exist with in-person working environments (Adkins, 2016). Expert analysts who study employee engagement stated that as the numbers of remote workers increase, the levels of workplace engagement decrease (Gallup, 2015). The amount of research that explains why engagement decreases among remote workers is minimal (Dvorak & Sasaki, 2017).

Many organizational leaders feel pressured to join the virtual work revolution to remain competitive in their respective marketplaces (Petrone, 2015). In doing so, leaders may sacrifice certain parts of the corporate vision to meet the demands of their growing workforce (Petrone, 2015). Because of feeling pressured to offer or increase virtual work options, organizational leaders may not plan for or be aware of the apparent change in the dynamics that occur with remote workers (Ortner, 2015). When leaders enter the virtual working environment under duress, their lack of awareness and planning could arguably be the cause for them to retract or ban virtual work options. Retracting the remote option will be a disadvantage in a gowning remote revolutionary market.

Wagner (2016) concluded that there is a correlation between years of service, colleague social influence, and the success of a remote worker. Scott, Dam, Paez, and Wilton (2012) concluded that employees who worked for the organization for an extended period and developed meaningful relationships with colleagues are better suited and more productive remote workers. The lack of depth of knowledge and information on how to engage employees remains challenging for managers who deal with traditional in-person and remote employees (Breevart et al., 2014).

Davis (2012) identified a significant difference in the engagement needs of traditional employee vs. remote employee (Davis, 2012). Dvorak and Sasaki (2017) stated that forty-five percent of U.S. workers are remote employees who work in another location other than their company location. One of the most significant barriers to telework is not having the necessary infrastructure (OPM, 2014). The workplace landscape is changing rapidly; each day brings about new technological advances that also bring about new challenges for leaders, employees, and organization alike to work harmoniously together (Mann & Harter, 2016).

Traditional Work Cultures Versus Remote Work Cultures

The current literature remains limited to the context of the traditional working environment and does not explicitly address remote workplace engagement (Fallon, 2015). The lack of a clear definition of workplace engagement for remote workers provides additional limitations because what data researchers should measure is unclear. The traditional working environment has a better understanding and definition than the emerging remote counterpart. In the traditional office, employees express and observe the definition of organizational engagement because of the characteristics of the environment (Ross, 2016). Organizational engagement in the remote work environment, where managers and employees may not have any regular face-to-face interaction, has no expression, and there are no defined methods of observing remote work engagement (Atwood, 2015).

Organizational leaders face new challenges in the modern workplace with remote workers and seem to have little to no training or tools to assist in their quest to be successful virtual leaders and managers (Elvekrog, 2015). The inability to physically and regularly observe the working conditions and behaviors of remote employees leaves leaders with limited information about their employees' workplace engagement, which often leads to a lack of trust between the leader and employee (Atwood, 2015). Leaders often think employees who work remotely have an unfair advantage over their in-office colleagues because they need not commute or attend impromptu meetings, assignments, and frequent workplace distractions that plague the traditional office (Chaney, 2016). Effective leaders, who understand the remote work environment can manage remote employees, promote organizational commitment, which leads to organizational growth.

A disparity between the requirements and expectations managers have of remote workers versus in-office workers who perform the same job functions has grown within the last decade; managers seem to have higher expectations of their remote workers (Fallon, 2014). If the work functions are the same, then the work location should not predicate a difference in the work expectation (Mejia, 2016). Remote workers are often distracted by activity occurring in their remote locations akin to on-site employees being distracted by activities in the physical plant (Michaels, 2016). Remote workers need to practice better self-discipline to remain productive out of the watchful eyes of supervisors (Adkins, 2016).

Organizational leaders of remote workers are handling their remote workers differently. Information on how to increase and sustain a remote environment of engagement and applicable policies, procedures, or training devised to centralize the knowledge of how to work most effectively with remote workers currently does not exist (Adkins, 2016). The sole use of technology to communicate is problematic as individuals attach their meanings, biases, and perceptions to written communication, thereby resulting in misinterpretation and compromised information (Nevogt, 2015). Technological options increased organizational leaders' ability to expand their workforce without expanding their physical workplace, so organizational leaders can build virtual teams without the cost of acquiring physical space (Parris, 2015). Although there is a cost saving in increasing a staff virtually instead of having them physically in the office, there is a cost associated with the rapidly changing remote work environment (Birnir, 2017).

Effective Strategies to Improve Remote Employees Engagement

Executive leaders use several strategies to improve remote employees' engagement. To get an understanding of the effect of the organizational vision on remote employees' engagement, the Musmar (2019) study included interviews 20 remote employees who are faculty members nationwide with experience of more than 2 years in remote educational settings. Below is the discussion of some of the strategies participants found to be useful to improve remote employees' engagement, including personal commitment, connection to mission and vision, and organizational culture.

Personal Commitment, Connection to Mission, and Vision Improved Remote Employees Engagement

The theme included word phrases, such as personal commitment, connection to mission and vision, engaged, and being a part of the organization. This theme emerged from all participants responding to all 4 questions. All of the participants used similar phrases when responding to the 4 interview questions. All participants felt the universities they worked for does an outstanding job of making them feel connected to the organization, their students, and colleagues.

The data from the Musmar (2019) study indicated that the participants felt their universities support them to take the initiative to make decisions to the best interest of the students and the university. The university's leadership team empowers faculties to make the right decision without waiting for approval from leadership and encourage faculties to collaborate with their peers to gain a better understanding of how to operate in their remote organizational environment. The leadership team of the universities provides faculty members with the tools they need to be successful and are also encouraged to seek leadership support when the need arises (Musmar, 2019). The findings that leadership support is important to improve remote employees' engagement are similar to the findings of Jordan, Werner, and Venter (2015) who also found that employees' engagement led to the superior performance of an organization.

Several participants made comments about the positive experiences they have had in feeling engaged and connected to their universities (Musmar, 2019). Participant # 7 described how he started as an adjunct faculty with his university and how he felt disengaged and disconnected at the beginning. He spoke with the leadership team, and they empowered him with their visionary initiatives to identify and ultimately create the work and role he wanted to do within his position. He stated, "The leadership team supported me with the tools to engage with my colleagues and helped me to connect my commitment to college mission and vision; a vision based on engaging faculties, leadership, and students in a positive social empowering environment" (Musmar, 2019). The leadership support example is one of the many examples reported from the participants that allude to patterns of positive connections associated with feelings of engagement. In the context of this study, utilizing personal commitment to the organizational vision and the connection to the organizational mission might improve remote employee's engagement.

Open and Friendly Principles Increased Remote Employees Engagement

The data from the Musmar (2019) study indicated that organizational leaders provide employees with the tools to be successful in an open and friendly way. Participants provided incidents in which they felt like they were working in a family and friendly environment. Participant # 13 is a university president; he stated that he created an engaging environment where he and his team felt like they were a family. The participant vision and claim appear valid according to the data, and participants' responses to this regard. All participants provided multiple incidents where they felt like their working environment was a friendly and a family- like with their coworkers (Musmar, 2019).

Participant # 2 provided a detailed account of what it meant to him to work in a family-like environment. He shared with his colleagues that his son was sick for a prolonged time and had to go through several hospitalizations. His co-workers, leadership team, and the president all personally contacted him to see if he and his son were ok. Every time his son return home, a bouquet of roses from the colleagues will be home waiting for him as a gesture during that ordeal. Participant #2 said he appreciated this gesture and concern he received from his family-like organization (Musmar, 2019). The findings that family environment is important to improve remote employees' engagement are similar to the findings of Adkins (2016), who also found that family environment created commitment and passion and a profound connection to the organization.

Many participants mentioned how the leadership teams encourage them to recommend people for vacant positions. The university president stated that engaged employees are the best lead for future employees. He encourages his employees to recommend friends if they feel they would be a good fit for the job. Participant #11 stated that the work environment is a family-like to him that keeps him motivated, engaged, and entertained. All participants mentioned that their colleges provide a specific chat feature for employees. The chat feature allows employees to converse with one another throughout their workday to keeps them socially engaged with each other. Participants discussed that they use this feature for work and personal socializing events. Participant #15 said that the chat feature is our virtual office, which is equal to the traditional office (Musmar, 2019).

Work-Life Balance and Social Interaction Promote Remote Employees Engagement

This theme emerged from all participants experiences of the work-life balance. Many participants mentioned how working remotely provides work-life flexibility. Participant #17 discussed how the flexibilities of working remotely are critical to her because she is a single mother. She mentioned how working remotely enabled her to keep up with her children needs and activities; a responsibility that she would not be able to carry work in a traditional office. She stated, "Working remotely allows me to do what I need to do at any given time; I take care of my family and work at my convenient time. I am so grateful for this work-life balance and flexibility." The findings that work-life balance is important to improve remote employees' engagement are similar to the findings of Chaney (2016) who also found that traditional office is time determent for meetings, assignments, and frequent workplace distractions that remote employees do not experience which lead to flexible time for work-life management.

All participant also mentioned social interaction through several office meeting events as key engagement events. Every participant considered these events as potent social and interpersonal events. Participants felt that these events allow everyone in the organization to engage face-to-face. Participant #5 mentioned that he worked for 10 months remotely; interacting with team members, but the meeting event enabled him to engage with his team members in person. Participant #10 stated, "By the time I entered the meeting event, I felt comfortable with everyone like I knew them personally like we are friends, and family." Several participants considered social interaction events as a smart engagement strategy for remote employees. Participant #13 stated that he attends all meeting events personally because he believes that social interaction is one of the most effective strategies in improving remote employees' engagement (Musmar, 2019).

Conclusion

Organizational leaders can improve remote employees engagement by using personal commitment, connection to mission and vision, open and friendly principles, work-life balance, and social interaction strategies. The strategies shared by participants might help organizational leaders increase productivity and profitability, promote organizational commitment, which leads to organizational growth. Educational organizations leaders need to consider and implement the above strategies as a way to improve organizational performance in their organizations. Implementing these strategies is less expensive than the costs associated with employees turnover. Therefore, recommendations include that organizational leaders use the findings and recommendations of this study to gain new insight into remote employees engagement strategies shared by experienced professionals. Organizational leaders who can use a refractive thinking approach in the implementation of effective organizational vision strategies might bring long-term success to their organizations.

THOUGHTS FROM THE ACADEMIC ENTREPRENEUR

The problem to be solved:

- Improving the employee's engagement in the remote environment

- Improving organizations' performance by applying the required strategies

The goals:

- Exploring the effect of the organizational vision on maintaining, strengthening, or eroding the remote workplace engagement

- Improving organizational performance through engagement

The questions to ask:

- What strategies do you use to improve remote employee's engagement?

- What strategies were most effective in improving remote employees' engagement?

- What are a few positive outcomes from using the identified strategies for improving engagement?

- What assessments do you use to assess the remote employee's engagement?

Today's Business Application:

- Effective leaders who understand the remote work environment can increase productivity and profitability, promote organizational commitment, which leads to organizational growth.

- The future of the remote work environment depends on leaders' ability to keeping the employees' engaged.

- Visionary leaders can increase organizational productivity and performance.

REFERENCES

Adkins, A. (2017). *Employee engagement in U.S. stagnant in 2015.* Retrieved from http://www.gallup.com/poll/188144/employee-engagement-stagnant-2015.aspx

Al Saifi, S. A. (2015). Positioning organisational culture in knowledge management research. *Journal of Knowledge Management, 19*(2), 164–189. doi:10.1108/jkm-07-2014-0287

Alvesson, M., & Sveningsson, S. (2015). *Changing organizational culture: Cultural change work in progress.* New York, NY: Routledge.

Anitha, J. (2014). Determinants of employee engagement and their impact on employee performance. *International Journal of Productivity and Performance Management, 63*(3), 308–323. doi:10.1108/ijppm-01-2013-0008

Anitha, J., & Aruna, M. (2016). Enablers of employee engagement of gen y at the workplace with reference to automobile sector. *Amnity Journal of Training and Development. 1*(1), 93–108. doi:10.4018/978-1-5225-0764-2.les2

Aon (2015). *2015 trends in global employee engagement.* Retrieved from http://www.aon.com/attachments/human-capital-consulting/2015-Trends-in-Global-Employee-Engagement-Report.pdf

Atwood, S. (2015). From a distance. *Smart Business Northern California, 8*(9), 6.

Azanza, G., Moriano, J. A., & Molero, F. (2013). Authentic leadership and organizational culture as drivers of employees' job satisfaction. *Revista de Psicología del Trabajo y de las Organizaciones, 29*(2), 45–50.

Benn, S., Dunphy, D., & Griffiths, A. (2014). *Organizational change for corporate sustainability.* London, England: Routledge.

Breevaart, K., Bakker, A., Hetland, J., Demerouti, E., Olsen, O. K., & Espevik, R. (2014). Daily transactional and transformational leadership and daily employee engagement. *Journal of Occupational and Organizational Psychology, 87*(1), 138–157. doi:10.1111/joop.12041

Birnir, A. (2017). *Ten reasons working remotely is even better than you thought it was.* Retrieved from https://www.themuse.com/advice/10-reasons-working-remotelyis-even-better-than-you-thought-it-was

Brio, M. (2014). Telecommuting is the future of work. *Forbes.* Retrieved from http://www.forbes.com

Cao, Z., Huo, B., Li, Y., & Zhao, X. (2015). The impact of organizational culture on supply chain integration: A contingency and configuration approach. *Supply Chain Management, 20*(1), 24. doi:10.1108/scm-11-2013-0426

Chaney, P. (2016). *Keep it down. Employees rank workplace distractions as biggest beef.* Retrieved from https://smallbiztrends.com/2016/06/how-to-get-rid-of-workplacedistractions.html

Colletta, J. B., Hoffman, J., Stone, K., & Bennett, N. (2016). *Assessing the relationship between partner perceptions and employee commitment to company.* Retrieved from http://www.swamfbd.org/uploads/SWAM_2016_Proceedings.pdf#page=71

Crawford, E. R., Rich, B. L., Buckman, B., & Bergeron, J. (2014). The antecedents and drivers of employee engagement. *Employee Engagement in Theory and Practice, 57*–81. doi:10.4324/9780429447419-7

Davis, R. (2012). *An investigation of the relationship between workplace isolation and engagement among teleworkers.* (Doctoral dissertation). Available from Pro-Quest Dissertations and Theses database. (UMI No. 3253217)

De Menezes, L. M., & Kelliher, C. (2016). Flexible working, individual performance, and employee attitudes: Comparing formal and informal arrangements. *Human Resource Management. 56,* 1051–1070. doi:10.1002/hrm.21822

Dvorak, N., & Sasaki, J. (2017). *Employees at home: Less engaged.* Retrieved from http://www.gallup.com/businessjournal/207539/employees-home-lessengaged.aspx/banner.html

Elvekrog, J. (2015). *5 ways to ensure remote workers feel part of the team.* Retrieved from https://www.entrepreneur.com/article/243795

Fallon, N. (2014). *No face time? No problem: How to keep virtual workers engaged.* Retrieved from http://www.businessnewsdaily.com/7228-engaging-remoteemployees.html

Fuller, R. (2014). *A primer on measuring employee engagement.* Retrieved from https://hbr.org/2014/11/a-primer-on-measuring-employee-engagement

Gallup. (2017). *State of the American workplace report.* Retrieved from http://www.gallup.com/reports/199961/state-american-workplace-report-2017.aspx?utm_source=SOAW&utm_campaign=StateofAmericanWorkplace&utm_medium=2013SOAWreport

Hackbarth, N. (2017). *Want to increase employee engagement? Hold managers accountable.* Retrieved from https://www.td.org/Publications/Blogs/Human Capital-Blog/2017/02/Want-to-Increase-Employee-Engagement-Hold-Managers -Accountable

Jordan, P. J., Werner, A., & Venter, D. (2015). Achieving excellence in private intensive care units: The effect of transformational leadership and organisational culture on organisational change outcomes. *SA Journal of Human Resource Management, 13*(1), 1–10. doi:10.4102/sajhrm.v13i1.707

Kahn, W. (1990). Psychological conditions of personal engagement and disengagement at work. *Academy of Management Journal, 33,* 692–724.

Klein, H. J., Polin, B., & Leigh Sutton, K. (2015). Specific onboarding practices for the socialization of new employees. *International Journal of Selection and Assessment, 23*(3), 263–283. doi:10.1111/ijsa.12113

Mann, A., & Adkins, A. (2017). *How engaged is your remote workforce?* Retrieved from http://www.gallup.com/businessjournal/206180/engaged-remote-workforce.aspx

Mann, A. & Harter, J. (2016). *The worldwide engagement crisis*. Retrieved from http://www.gallup.com/businessjournal/188033/worldwide-employeeengagement-crisis.aspx

McGregor, L., & Doshi, N. (2015). *How company culture shapes employee motivation*. Retrieved from https://hbr.org/2015/11/how-company-culture-shapes-employee motivation

Mejia, M. (2016). *How to include remote employees in your company culture*. Retrieved from https://www.eremedia.com/tlnt/how-to-include-remote-employees -in-yourcompany-culture/

Michaels, L. (2016). *Managing a remote team? Your employees may feel lonely and isolated*. Retrieved from http://yfsmagazine.com/2016/06/23/managing-a-remoteteam-your-employees-may-feel-lonely-and-isolated/

Naqshbandi, M., Kaur, S., Sehgal, R. & Subramaniam, I. (2015). Organizational culture profile of Malaysian high-tech industries. *Asia-Pacific Journal of Business Administration, 7*(1), 2–19. doi:10.1108/APJBA-08–2013–0088

Nevogt, D. (2015). *How to retain your a-player remote workers*. Retrieved from http://blog.hubstaff.com/remote-employee-retention-strategies/

Nickson, C. (2016). *Technology & the way we work*. Retrieved from http://www.atechnologysociety.co.uk/technology-way-we-work.html

Nor, H. A., Shamsuddin, A., & Wahab, E. (2015). Does organizational culture mediate the relationship between transformational leadership and organizational commitment. *International Journal of Organizational Leadership, 4*(1), 18–32. doi:10.33844/ijol.2015.60344

O'Brien, P. (2014). *Why strong employee/employer relationship is important and how to achieve this*. Retrieved from http://www.business2community.com/strategy/strong-employeeemployerrelationship-important-achieve-0876781#ecuYhg-J4YxuJJbKq.97

Office of Personnel Management (OPM). (2014). *2013 status of telework in the government*. Retrieved from http://www.opm.gov

Ortner, M. (2015). *Why telecommuting can be dangerous for your company culture*. Retrieved from http://www.fastcompany.com/3040750/why-telecommuting-canbe -dangerous-for-your-company-culture

Parris, J. (2015). *Six interesting benefits of remote work*. Retrieved from https://remote.co/6-interesting-benefits-of-remote-work/

Peh, C. & Wee, A. (2015). *Gen Z: Redefining the workplace?* Retrieved from http://www.cnbc.com/2015/01/15/gen-z-redefining-the-workplace.html

Petrone, P. (2015). *Why allowing telecommuting is (and isn't) a good idea*. Retrieved from https://www.linkedin.com/pulse/why-allowing-telecommuting-isnt -goodidea-paul-petrone

Piaget, J. (2013). Understanding culture and cultural interfaces. *International Management Ethics*, 11–39. doi:10.1017/cbo9780511975585.002

Pinho, J. C., Ana, P. R., & Dibb, S. (2014). The role of corporate culture, market orientation and organisational commitment in organisational performance. *The Journal of Management Development, 33*(4), 374–398. doi:10.1108/ JMD-03-2013-0036

Reilly, R. (2014). *Five ways to improve employee engagement now.* http://www. gallup.com/businessjournal/166667/five-ways-improve-employeeengagement.aspx

Reynolds, B. (2011). *Telecommuting or teleworking-what's the difference?* Retrieved from https://www.flexjobs.com/blog/post/telecommuting-or-telework-whats -thedifference/

Roark, P. (2013). Employee engagement. *Leadership Excellence, 30*(9), 25–26.

Ross, E. (2016). *How leadership has changed because of technology.* Retrieved from https://www.virgin.com/entrepreneur/how-leadership-has-changed-because technology

Saks, A. M. (2006). Antecedents and consequences of employee engagement. *Journal of Managerial Psychology, 21,* 600–619.

Scott, D., Dam, I., Páez, A. & Wilton, R. (2012). Investigating the effects of social influence on the choice to telework. *Environment and Planning, 44,* 1016–1031. doi:10.1068/a43223

Smith, A., & Garcia, A. (2016). *Chipotle to close all restaurants on Feb 8 for food safety meeting.* Retrieved from http://money.cnn.com/2016/01/15/news/companies/ chipotle-food-safety-meeting/

Solomon, M. (2014). *To build a powerful company culture, create a powerful orientation process.* Retrieved from http://www.forbes.com/sites/micahsolomon/2014/11/07/to-build-a-powerfulcompany-culture-create-a-powerful-orientation-process/#269f7d863ed7

Sutherland, L. (2015). *How to combat loneliness, and disconnection as a remote worker.* Retrieved from https://remote.co/how-to-combat-loneliness-and -disconnection-asa-remote-worker/

Traphagan, J. (2015). *Why company culture is a misleading term.* Retrieved from https://hbr.org/2015/04/why-company-culture-is-a-misleading-term

Tugend, A. (2018). It's clearly undefined, but telecommuting is fast on the rise. *New York Times.* Retrieved from http://www.nytimes.com

Turker, D., & Altuntas, C. (2015). A longitudinal study on newcomers' perception of organisational culture. *Education & Training, 57*(2), 130–147. doi:10.1108/ et-02-2013-0022

Wagner, R. (2016). The 7 lessons of Marisa Mayer's loss of command at Yahoo. Retrieved from http://www.forbes.com/sites/roddwagner/2016/03/08/ the-sevenlessons-of-marissa-mayers-loss-of-command-at-yahoo/#60f77ddc36c3

About the Author...

Dr. Frank Musmar resides in Richardson, Texas. Dr. Frank is currently an adjunct professor at Louisiana International College and American Management and Technology University. Dr. Frank received his Doctorate of Business Administration (DBA) in Healthcare Management from Walden University in 2016, a Master of Science (MS) in Biotechnology Management from the University of Maryland in 2011 and Bachelor of Science (BS) in Agriculture from the University of Jordan in 1992.

Dr. Frank is the founder and the Lead Dissertations Consultant at *Editors Dissertations and Thesis,* founded on the ideals that helping students achieve their educational goals could bring positive social change.

Dr. Frank is also an active member of the Delta Mu Delta Honor Society and Golden Key International Honor Society.

He has published four journal publications: Factors Affecting Millennials Healthcare Employees Turnover, Job Embeddedness and Employee Retention in Healthcare, a Once-daily Oral Medication for Treatment of Cognitive Dysfunction in Down syndrome, and Financial Distress at Nonprofit Organizations. Additional work includes his dissertation: Financial Distress in the Health Care Business.

To reach Dr. Frank Musmar for information on professional editing or guest speaking, please visit his **websites:** http://www.editorsdissertationsandthesis.com or **e-mail:** frankmusmar@gmail.com

CHAPTER 3

The Good Organizational Citizen: Collectivist or Individualist?

Dr. Curtis Dale Curry

In modern organizations, what defines a good organizational citizen? How do leaders and HR professionals identify those good citizens? What benefits do good organizational citizens bring to organizations? The following chapter explores these questions.

This author blends two personal passions in the chapter: a lifelong pursuit of philosophy, specifically *eudaimonia,* the search for meaning, or *the good life,* with a nearly three decades-long career in global leadership development, intercultural communication, and organizational performance. Refractive thinkers ask the big questions, and the good life and the role of the good citizen certainly should qualify as big questions. This passion eventually led to the focus on two areas within the author's dissertation: a long-term career interest in supporting organizational performance and continued interest in eudaimonia, which led to organizational citizenship behavior, and individualism and collectivism, stemming from interest in cross-cultural training.

Because global organizations strive to increase productivity and decrease costs, organizational leaders work assiduously to do more with less by acquiring more efficient methods of operating and leveraging existing resources. A major challenge to these efforts in the Americas, Europe, and Asia is rapidly changing demographics: declining fertility rates in these regions coupled with millions of aging Baby Boomers retiring over the next two decades (Economist, 2009). Organizations continue to respond by maximizing existing employees' contributions (Cates, Mathis, & Randle, 2010; Dávila, Celeste, & Finkelstein, 2011; Hoffman, Blair, Meriac, & Woehr, 2007; Zhang, Liao, &Zhao, 2011). Organizational citizenship behavior (OCB) is of central interest as a possible path for increasing productivity and reducing costs.

While OCB was initially thought of as discretionary job behavior that promoted organizational effectiveness (Moorman & Blakely, 1995), after researchers discovered that some individuals viewed OCB as a part of their job (Podsakoff et al., 2009), the concept was re-defined by Organ (1997) as "performance that supports the social and psychological environment in which task performance takes place" (p. 95). OCB impacts positively a number of organizational effectiveness measures, including productivity (Podsakoff et al., 2009; Whitman ,Van Rooy, & Viswesvaran, 2010), increased efficiency, reduced costs, increased customer satisfaction, and reduced absenteeism (Podsakoff et al., 2009), job satisfaction (Bateman & Organ, 1983; Hoffman et al., 2007; Whitman et al., 2010), and finally, happier, more enthusiastic employees, better quality work, and a positive impact on the organization's bottom line (Derderian, 2012). Clearly, if OCB can positively impact so many areas key to organizational success, organizational citizenship is an area that should significantly interest leaders.

The two types of OCB to explore included OCB directed at individuals (OCBI) and OCB directed at helping the organization, OCBO. McShane and Von Glinow (2013) noted that OCBO includes behaviors focused on helping the organization such as "supporting the company's public image, taking discretionary action to help the organization avoid potential problems, and offering ideas beyond those required for the job" (p. 38). OCBI, focusing on helping the individuals in organizations (thereby indirectly supporting the organization) include "assisting co-workers with their work problems, adjusting work schedules to accommodate coworkers, [and] showing genuine courtesy toward coworkers and sharing work resources" (McShane & Von Glinow, 2013, p. 38). The Curry (2016) study measured both types of OCB using Williams and Anderson's (1991) instrument.

Promoting OCB clearly affords manifold benefits to organizations. Two relevant questions to ask are who is likeliest to perform OCB, and the second question, how and if OCB can be encouraged in employees. The task in the Curry (2016) dissertation was to conduct research related to the 'who' question and the last part of this chapter will offer some preliminary thoughts on the *if* and *how* OCB might be promoted question.

With a background in cross-cultural communication, the purpose was to know if collectivists, given their group orientation, might be more likely to exhibit OCBs than individualists. Individualism is a cultural pattern where individuals view themselves as independent and pursue individual goals and collectivism is a cultural pattern where individuals see themselves as part of an in-group and pursue group goals. In the course of the Curry (2016) study, the author focused on two forms of individualism and collectivism described below.

In *Exploring Vertical and Horizontal Dimensions of Individualism and Collectivism as Predictors of Organizational Citizenship Behavior,* the Curry (2016) study sought to determine whether two forms of individualism (vertical and horizontal) or collectivism (vertical and horizontal) could predict OCB directed towards individuals (OCBI) or OCB directed towards the organization (OCBO). Individuals who score high in vertical collectivism (VC) view themselves as part of an in-group, focus on in-group goals, and accept hierarchy and inequality (Singelis et al., 1995). Horizontal collectivists (HC) value equality and view themselves as members of an in-group of similar interdependent individuals (Singelis et al., 1995). Vertical individualism (VI) is a cultural pattern where individuals value competition and see themselves as autonomous from the group; they tend to focus on achieving individual goals, are self-reliant, and expect inequality (Singelis et al., 1995). Finally, in the cultural pattern of horizontal individualism (HI), individuals value equality and are self-reliant, but view themselves as autonomous from the group (Singelis et al., 1995), In the study (2016), the author discovered that both forms of collectivism (VC and HC) and vertical individualism were significant predictors of OCB directed towards the individual (OCBI). The author used Cronbach's alpha to determine the reliability of each scale. The original OCBO scale used in the research (Williams & Anderson, 1991) proved unreliable, so a combined OCBI and OCBO scale, which was reliable (labeled OCB-Total) was used. Both horizontal collectivism and vertical collectivism were significant predictors of the combined OCB scale, OCB-Total, but neither form of individualism was significant In the case of OCBI and OCB-Total, my research, consistent with several other studies discussed below, indicated that collectivists were more likely to engage in OCB than individualists (Dávila & Finkelstein, 2011; Felfe et al., 2008; Liu & Fellows, 2011; Moorman & Blakely, 1995).

Organizational Citizenship Behavior

"The good life is the chief end, both for the community
as a whole and for each of us individually."
—ARISTOTLE, POLITICS III, CHAPTER 6.

In the *Nicomachean Ethics,* Aristotle (2000) discussed the importance of leading a virtuous, good life (eudaimonia), and discussed the role of the state in man's pursuit of living the 'good life' in the *Politics* (Aristotle & Barker, 1980). The very purpose of the *polis* included the view of promoting *the good life* "while [the polis] grows for the sake of mere life (and is so far, at that stage, still short of full self-sufficiency), it exists (when once it is fully grown) for the sake of the good life" (Aristotle & Barker, 1980, p. 5). Aristotle also outlined the meaning of citizenship and the *good citizen* in the *Politics* (1980). Aristotle argued that the life of the citizen is bound with that of the *polis*. The *good citizen* was one who understood his obligations to the polis and also shared "in the civic life of ruling and being ruled in turn" (Aristotle & Barker, 1980, p. 134). A good citizen not only possessed virtue, but also acted on it by participating actively in the life of the state.

While Aristotle was the catalyst for my initial interest in citizenship, Bateman and Organ (1983) were the first modern social scientists to delve into citizenship behavior in organizations. Bateman and Organ (1983) defined citizenship behaviors as ones that "include any of those gestures (often taken for granted) that lubricate the social machinery of the organization but that do not directly in here in the usual notion of task performance" (p. 588). Like the obligations for Aristotle's good citizens, organizational citizenship behavior (OCB) is not considered behavior that is mandated or outlined in a job description, but rather is discretionary behavior that supported organizational effectiveness (Moorman & Blakely, 1995).

The Curry (2016) study used the Williams and Anderson's (1991) approach that included the two types of OCBs discussed earlier: organizational citizenship behavior directed at individual coworkers (OCBI) and organizational citizenship behavior that directly benefited the organization (OCBO). OCBI items from the survey include going out of one's way to help new coworkers and taking time to listen to coworkers' problems (Williams & Anderson, 1991). OCBO included areas such as attendance at work being better than average and taking undeserved work breaks (Williams & Anderson, 1991).

Social Exchange Theory and OCB

Aristotle declared that man was a political animal and entered associations with others that grew into the *polis,* to allow men to attain the good life. The creators of social exchange theory, Homans (1958) and Blau (2002) also include descriptions of individuals entering into associations, and their theory undergirds organizational citizenship. Similar to economic exchange theory, Blau (2002) and Homans (1958) in describing social exchange theory argue that when individuals engage in relationships, they exchange something of value (both material, such as goods, and non-material, such as advice) in return for receiving something of value from the other. Social exchange between individuals creates mutual obligations. Homans (1958) offered the formula Profit = Reward—Cost, explaining that all three include not only monetary costs and rewards, but also status, extra responsibility, and peace of mind. According to Homans (1958), when the costs are too high, one party might eschew giving altogether. Individuals are motivated to enter into social relationships with others not by merely calculating gains and losses in simple economic terms, but rather by a calculus that includes more complex factors such as gaining status and avoiding worry.

Blau (2002) stressed that while obligations were reciprocal, unlike economic exchange, they were unspecified. He defined social exchange as "voluntary actions of individuals that are motivated by the returns they are expected to bring and typically do in fact bring from others" (Blau, 2002, pp. 80–81). The social exchange is voluntary, based on future expected rewards such as recognition, social approval, and extrinsic rewards. Blau provided an example of a manager encouraging an employee to work hard to improve the company's financial state in exchange for future rewards such as increased status or social approval that validates the employee's personal values.

Employees voluntarily engage in OCB, and social exchange

theorists suggest that the employees would do so in exchange for intangible rewards such as recognition and social approval. Philipp (2012) found that employees were indeed more willing to engage in OCB to promote the interests of the organization when they had a long-term relationship with it. Trust is a key element of social exchange that was identified by Organ and Konovsky (1989): "So long as the individual can sustain an attitude of trust in the long-term fairness of the organization in the relationship, he or she need not worry about the recompense for this or that specific OCB gesture" (p. 162). If one party violates trust, the relationship devolves into a *quid pro quo* status because fairness is an implicit factor at work in social exchange theory. Cho (2013) found that OCB increases when individuals receive respect: "These results are consistent with social exchange theory in that those who received respect and admiration reciprocated by engaging in OCB. The combination of lacking status and having power frees individuals from returning behavior that is neither formally required nor rewarded" (pp. 20–21). The Organ and Konovsky (1989), Philipp (2012), and Cho (2013) studies support social exchange theory.

Individualism / Collectivism

After extensive travels in the United States, Alexis de Toqueville (1966), in his trenchant observations on American life and politics, introduced the concept of individualism in his *Democracy in America*. Toqueville described individualism as "a mature and calm feeling, which disposes each member of the community to sever himself from the mass of his fellows and to draw apart with his family and his friends, so that after he has thus formed a little circle of his own, he willingly leaves society at large to itself" (p. 98). Toqueville believed that individualism was the natural outcome of a democratic society, arguing that once individuals in the United States achieved the education and economic means, they became self-sufficient: "They owe nothing to any man, they expect nothing from any man; they acquire the habit of always considering themselves as standing alone, and they are apt to imagine that their whole destiny is in their own hands" (p. 99). Toqueville's nineteenth century insights on US Americans would point the way for social scientists who would resurrect and refine the concept of individualism a century and a half later.

Geert Hofstede (2001) took up the theme of individualism with his trail-blazing cross-cultural work at IBM. His focus was national culture, which he eventually referred to as 'software of the mind' (Hofstede, Hofstede, & Minkov, 2010). Hofstede's research from 1967 and 1973 drew data from over 100,000 participants from 72 countries in 20 languages, and his studies popularized the terms individualism and collectivism Hofstede organized national cultures along a continuum, from nations high in individualism, like the United States and Australia to countries on the other end of the continuum high in collectivism like China and Colombia. Nations high in collectivism are, "societies in which people form birth onward are integrated into strong, cohesive in-groups, which throughout people's lifetime continue to protect them in exchange for unquestioning loyalty" (Hofstede et al., 2010, p. 92). Collectivist societies exhibit loyalty to in-groups and focus on 'we' goals as opposed to 'I' goals, and view self in interdependent terms (Hofstede et al., 2010). Individualists focus on their individual goals, immediate family, apply universal standards to all, focus more on individual achievement and individual "I" goals and view the self as an independent (Hofstede et al., 2010).

Research indicates that individualism and collectivism vary both across individuals and cultures (Felfe et al., 2008; Noordin & Jusoff, 2010; Oyserman & Lee, 2008; Singelis, Triandis, Bhawuk, & Gelfand, 1995; Taras et al., 2014), so I decided to use a multidimensional construct of the dimensions created by Singelis, Triandis, Bhawuk and Gelfand (1995) instead of Hofstede's (2001) bipolar construct of individualism and collectivism. In an extensive review of the literature, Triandis (1996) identified horizontal and vertical dimensions of individualism and collectivism. The horizontal dimension focused on equality and the vertical focused on the acceptance of hierarchy/inequality (Triandis, 1996).

Horizontal collectivism (HC) is a cultural pattern where equality is valued and individuals see themselves as part of an interdependent in-group and therefore focus on achieving in-group goals (Singelis, Triandis, Bhawuk, & Gelfand, 1995). Vertical collectivism (VC) like HC values the in-group, so the individual focuses on in-group goals, though accepts greater hierarchy and inequality. Vertical individualism (VI) is a cultural pattern where individuals view themselves as autonomous from the in-group, value hierarchy and accept greater inequality, individuals exhibiting this preference pursue individual goals, value competition, and they are self-reliant. Horizontal individualism values equality and self-reliance and sees the self as autonomous from the in-group. The following table reproduced from my dissertation summarizes the differences and similarities between the horizontal and vertical dimensions of individualism and collectivism.

TABLE 1. SUMMARY OF SINGELIS ET AL. (1995) VERTICAL AND HORIZONTAL DIMENSIONS OF INDIVIDUALISM AND COLLECTIVISM

INDIVIDUALISM		COLLECTIVISM	
Horizontal	Vertical	Horizontal	Vertical
Equality	Inequality accepted	Equality	Inequality accepted
Independent self	Independent self	Interdependent self	Interdependent self
Similar to others	Different from others	Similar to others	Different from others
Self-reliant	Competition	Common goals	In-group goals above individual goals
Do "own thing"	Acquire status	Do not submit to authority easily	
Autonomous self	Individual goals		Competition with out groups
I'm unique	Be the best	Identify with in-group	

Singelis et al. (1995) speculated on national archetypes for each dimension. HC might be common for Israel where the kibbutz would represent collectivism, though equality among citizens is a feature of Israeli society (Singelis et al., 1995). VC would be common for traditional Indian villages where deference to village elders would be an important feature in a more collectivist society (Singelis et al., 1995). HI would likely be characteristic of highly individualist Australia where equality is central and 'tall poppies' who have high status would find disapproval (Singelis et al., 1995). VI would be more characteristic of the highly individualist U.S. Americans and France where inequality might be expected to be a natural outcome of a competitive society, but individualism also was greatly valued (Singelis et al., 1995).

Using a sample of employees from business organizations in diverse central and south Florida, the purpose of my quantitative study was to see if any of the four forms could predict OCB directed towards individuals (OCBI) or organizations (OCBO). Both forms of collectivism predicted OCBI. This finding was consistent with several earlier studies showing that collectivism could predict the performance of organizational citizenship behavior in certain contexts (Dávila & Finkelstein, 2011; Liu & Fellows, 2011; Moorman & Blakely, 1995). One reason may be that since collectivists value in-group goals above individual goals, they may be more likely to engage in OCB to further the interests of the collective (Dávila & Finkelstein, 2011; Felfe et al., 2008; Liu & Fellows, 2011; Moorman & Blakely, 1995).

While the OCBI scale used in the study was reliable, a Cronbach's alpha of .354 was obtained for the OCBO scale, so it could not be used. When, however, by combining the two OCB scales into a single construct comprised of 14 items, reliability improved to 0.705. The author used this combined scale along with the OCBI scale in the study and labeled the combined scale OCB-Total. Both forms of collectivism predicted the performance of OCB-Total. Both forms of collectivism, along with vertical individualism also predicted OCBI.

Conclusion and Implications for Our Business Readers

A major focus of organizational leaders and human resource development professionals is to improve both individual and organizational performance, and research suggests that employees who engage in OCB benefit the organization in many ways including improved performance, increased efficiency, lower costs, higher quality work, increased customer satisfaction, happier, more enthusiastic employees and lower turnover. As Hoffman et al. (2007) noted, "In a business environment characterized by flattened organizational structures, competition from international economies, and increased employee autonomy and responsibility, the performance of discretionary work behaviors has been deemed essential to effective organizational functioning" (p. 555). For organizational leaders, it makes sense to promote OCB for the manifold benefits organizations enjoy when their employees engage in organizational citizenship behavior. There seem to be two ways to do this: find ways to encourage OCB in employees who may be less likely to engage in the behavior or select candidates who are more likely to engage in OCB. While the latter suggestion carries both practical and legal barriers, understanding better those factors that encourage OCB in collectivists and possibly vertical individualists makes sense. Why are these employees more likely to engage in OCB? What are factors that influence employees who are less likely to demonstrate OCB? What are differences in motivation for employees who engage in either OCBI or OCBO, or both?

While the Curry (2016) study did demonstrate a significant positive relationship between vertical individualism and OCBI, it also followed the pattern of several other studies that showed collectivism predicting OCB (in the current study, both forms of collectivism predicted OCBI and OCB-Total). Dávila and Finkelstein (2011), Felfe et al. (2008), Liu and Fellows (2011) and Moorman and Blakely (1995) found that collectivists were more likely to engage in organizational citizenship behavior than individualists. Only one, Finkelstein (2012), using a sample of undergraduate students, showed a significant positive correlation between individualism (in this case as a single construct) and OCBO.

Because the Williams and Anderson's (1991) OCBO scale proved unreliable, researchers should continue investigating other measures of OCBO. The current author chose the Williams and Anderson (1991) framework for a variety of reasons. First, Podsakoff et al. (2009) found in a large meta-study that Williams and Anderson was a comprehensive framework that incorporated most other OCB constructs. Further, Organ (1997) argued that the model was useful because of looking at both OCBI and OCBO.

Cho (2013), Dávila and Finkelstein (2012), and Finkelstein (2012) used Lee and Allen's (2002) 16-item OCBI-OCBO scales. OCBO items include "attend functions that are not required but help the organizational image," "defend the organization when other employees criticize it," and "express loyalty towards the organization" (Lee & Allen, 2002, p. 142). These items may better capture OCBO than the Williams and Anderson framework. Lee and Allen's (2002) scales showed reliabilities of .88 for OCBO and .83 (OCBI).

Because there are only a handful of studies exploring national cultures, more cross-cultural studies investigating relationships between the vertical and horizontal dimensions of individualism and collectivism and OCBO / OCBI are needed. Noordin and Hamali (2009), focusing on Malaysian middle managers, discovered that employees who had westerners as leaders had higher levels of HI. Chiou (2001) in a study of Argentinian, Taiwanese, and U.S. students discovered, as one might expect, the Argentinians and Taiwanese scored higher in VC, the U.S. students were higher in HI, and the United States and Taiwanese students were higher in VI than the Argentinians. In a study conducted by Noordin and Jusoff (2010), results indicated that Australians scored higher in HI as might be expected but Malaysian managers scored higher in VI. Hofstede et al. (2010) clearly place Malaysia on the collectivist end of their individualism collectivism continuum. In another study focusing on Spaniards, Gouveia, Clemente and Espinosa (2003) found that while participants scored highest on HC, overall they were only slightly more collectivist than individualist. Both studies' authors argued that higher than expected individualism scores could be the result of a global tendency for societies, as they develop, to become more individualistic: "The development of a middle class presupposes social mobility and social mobility in turn leads to individualism" (Noordin & Jusoff, 2010, p. 168). In our rapidly globalizing business world, learning more about how the vertical and horizontal dimensions of individualism and collectivism relate to national cultures and the performance of OCB could help leaders and HR professionals better understand, and perhaps one day impact, the factors that make good organizational citizens.

THOUGHTS FROM THE ACADEMIC ENTREPRENEUR

The problem to be solved:

- Determining whether vertical individualism (VI), vertical collectivism (VC), horizontal individualism (HI), and horizontal collectivism (HC) could predict organizational citizenship behavior directed at individuals (OCBI) or organizations (OCBO).

The goals:

- Understand the importance of OCB, OCBI, and OCBO in effective organizational performance
- Conduct a quantitative study to determine if the various forms of individualism and collectivism impact the performance of OCB, OCBI and OCBO

The questions to ask:

- What are the different types of organizational citizenship behavior, and why are they so important to organizational functioning?
- Who is more likely to engage in organizational citizenship behavior, collectivists, or individualists?
- How can organizations encourage organizational citizenship behavior?

Today's Business Application:

- Employees who engage in organizational citizenship behaviors bring manifold benefits to organizations, including higher productivity, better customer service, lower costs, greater efficiency, lower turnover, happier employees and reduced turnover.
- Leaders who understand organizational citizenship behavior may be able to look for ways to encourage it.

REFERENCES

Aristotle. (2000). The Nicomachean ethics. Retrieved from http://classics.mit.edu/Aristotle/nicomachaen.mb.txtAristotle & Barker, E. (1962). *The politics of Aristotle*. New York, NY: Oxford University Press.

Aristotle & Barker, E. (1980). *The politics of Aristotle*. New York, NY: Oxford University Press.

Bateman, T. S., & Organ, D. W. (1983). Job satisfaction and the good soldier: The relationship between affect and employee "citizenship." *Academy of Management Journal, 26,* 587–595. doi:10.2307/255908

Blau, P. M. (2004). *Exchange and power in social life*. New Brunswick & London: Transaction Publishers.

Cates, D. A., Mathis, C. J., & Randle, N. W. (2010). A positive perspective of citizenship pressure among working adults. *Journal of Managerial Issues, 22,* 330–344, 284. Retrieved from https://www.jstor.org/journal/jmanaissues

Chiao, J. Y., Harada, T., Komeda, H., Li, Z., Mano, Y., Saito, D., & Iidaka, T. (2009). Neural basis of individualistic and collectivistic views of self. *Human Brain Mapping, 30,* 2813–2820. doi:10.1002/hbm.20707

Cho, Y. (2013). *Power, status, and organizational citizenship behavior* (Doctoral dissertation). Retrieved from http://digitallibrary.usc.edu/cdm/ref/collection/p15799coll3/id/294602

Curry, C.D. (2016). *Exploring vertical and horizontal dimensions of individualism and collectivism as predictors of organizational citizenship behavior*(Doctoral dissertation). Barry University, Miami, Florida.

Dávila, M. C. Celeste, D., & Finkelstein, M. A. (2011). Individualism/collectivism and organizational citizenship behavior. *Psicothema, 23,* 401–406. Retrieved from https://www.uniovido.net/reunido/index.php/PST/index

Derderian, V. (2012). Organizational citizenship. In R. K. Prescott (Ed.), *The encyclopedia of human resource management, Volume 1*. San Francisco, CA: Wiley & Sons.

Felfe, J., Yan, W., & Bend, S. (2008). The impact of individual collectivism on commitment and its influence on organizational citizenship behavior and turnover in three countries. *International Journal of Cross Cultural Management,* (8)2, 211–237. doi:10.1177/1470595808091790

Finkelstein, M. A. (2012). Individualism/collectivism and organizational citizenship behavior: An integrative framework. *Social Behavior and Personality, 40,* 1633–1643. doi:10.2224/sbp.2012.40.10.1633

Gouveia, V. V., Clemente, M., & Espinosa, P. (2003). The horizontal and vertical attributes of individualism and collectivism in a Spanish population. *The Journal of Social Psychology, 143*(1), 43–63. doi:10.1080/00224540309598430

Hoffman, B. J., Blair, C. A., Meriac, J. P., & Woehr, D. J. (2007). Expanding the criterion domain?: A quantitative review of the OCB literature. *Journal of Applied Psychology, 92*, 555–566. doi:10.1037/0021-9010.92.2.555

Hofstede, G. (2001). *Culture's consequences: Comparing values, behaviors, institutions, and organizations across nations.* Thousand Oaks, CA: Sage Publications.

Hofstede, G., Hofstede, G. J., & Minkov, M. (2010). *Cultures and organizations: Software of the mind* (3rd ed.). New York, NY: McGraw Hill.

Homans, G. C. (1958). Social behavior as exchange. *American Journal of Sociology, 63*, 597–606. doi:10.1086/222355

McShane, S. L., & Von Glinow, M. A. (2013). *Organizational behavior* (6th ed.). New York, NY: McGraw-Hill / Irwin.

Moorman, R. H., & Blakely, G. L. (1995). Individualism—collectivism as an individual difference predictor of organizational citizenship behavior. *Journal of Organizational Behavior, 16*(2), 127–142. doi:10.1002/job.4030160204

Noordin, F., & Hamali, J. (2009). Individualism-collectivism and organizational value types: the case of Malaysian managers. *International Business and Economics Research Journal, 8*(4). doi:10.19030/iber.v8i4.3125

Noordin, F., & Jusoff, K. (2010). Individualism-collectivism and job satisfaction between Malaysia and Australia. *International Journal of Educational Management, 24*(2), 159–174. doi:10.1108/09513541011020963

Organ, D. (1997). Organizational citizenship behavior: It's construct clean-up time. *Human Performance, 10*(2), 85–97. doi:10.1207/s15327043hup1002_2

Organ, D. W., & Konovsky, M. (1989). Cognitive versus affective determinants of organizational citizenship behavior. *Journal of Applied Psychology, 74*(1), 157–164. doi:10.1037/0021-9010.74.1.157

Oyserman, D., & Lee, S. W. S. (2008). Does culture influence what and how we think?: Effects of priming individualism and collectivism. *Psychological Bulletin, 134*, 311–342. doi:10.1037/0033-2909.134.2.311

Philipp, B.L.U. (2012). *Psychological contracts in the workplace: Relationships among organizational commitment, organizational citizenship behaviors, and ethical leadership* (Doctoral dissertation). Retrieved from ProQuest Dissertations and Theses database. (UMI No. 3523554)

Podsakoff, N. P., Whiting, S. W., Podsakoff, P.M., & Blume, B. D. (2009). Individual- and organizational-level consequences of organizational citizenship behaviors: A meta-analysis. *Journal of Applied Psychology, 94*(1), 122–141. doi:10.1037/a0013079

Podsakoff, P. M., & MacKenzie, S. B. (1997). Impact of organizational citizenship behavior on organizational performance: A review and suggestion for future research. *Human Performance, 10*(2), 133. doi:10.1207/s15327043hup1002_5

Podsakoff, P. M., MacKenzie, S. B., Paine, J. B., & Bachrach, D. G. (2000).

Organizational citizenship behaviors: A critical review of the theoretical and empirical literature and suggestions for future research. *Journal of Management, 26,* 513–563. doi:10.1177/014920630002600307

Rousseau, J. J. (1973). *The social contract and discourses.* New York, NY: Everyman's Library.

Singelis, T. M., Triandis, H. C., Bhawuk, D. P. S., & Gelfand, M. (1995). Horizontal and vertical dimensions of individualism and collectivism: A theoretical and measurement refinement. *Cross-Cultural Research, 29*(3), 240–275. doi:10.1177/106939719502900302

The Economist. (2009, June 25). A survey of ageing populations: A slow-burning fuse. Retrieved from http://www.economist.com/node/13888045?story_id=13888045

Taras, V., Sarala, R., Muchinsky, P., Kemmelmeier, M. Singelis, T. M., Avsec, A. Coon, H. M., Dinnel, D, Gardner, W., Grace, S., Hardin, E., Hsu, S., Johnson, J. Aygün, Z.K., Kashima, E. S., Kolstad, A., Milfont, T. L., Oetzel, J., Okazaki, S., Probst, T. M., Sato, T, Shafiro, S, Schwartz, S. J. & Sinclair, H. C. (2014). Opposite ends of the same stick?: Multi-method test of the dimensionality of individualism and collectivism. *Journal of Cross-Cultural Psychology, 45*(2) 213–245. doi:10.1177/0022022113509132

Tocqueville, A. D., & Reeve, H. (1966). *Democracy in America* (Rev. ed., v. II). New York, NY: Random House.

Triandis, H. C. (1996). The psychological measurement of cultural syndromes. *American Psychologist, 51,* 407–415. doi:10.1037/0003–066X.51.4.407

Whitman, D. S., Van Rooy, D. L., & Viswesvaran, C. (2010). Satisfaction, citizenship behaviors, and performance in work units: A meta-analysis of collective construct relations. *Personnel Psychology, 63*(1), 41–81. doi:10.1111/j.1744–6570.2009.01162.x

Williams, L. J., & Anderson, S. E. (1991). Job satisfaction and organizational commitment as predictors of organizational citizenship and in-role behaviors. *Journal of Management, 17,* 601–617. doi:10.1177/014920639101700305

Zhang, Y., Liao, J., & Zhao, J. (2011). Research on the organizational citizenship behavior continuum and its consequences. *Frontiers of Business Research in China, 5,* 364–379. doi:10.1007/s11782–011–0135–2

About the Author . . .

Dr. Curtis D. Curry lives on Florida's Space Coast. President of Quality Learning International, Dr. Curry has over 25 years of leadership experience working with global organizations in the human and organizational performance improvement field. He has trained over 40,000 leaders and individual contributors from 200+ organizations including Ricoh, Harris, United Space Alliance, Honeywell Aerospace, Roche do Brasil, BHP Chile, Kraft Brazil, Colgate, and Peabody Energy. Dr. Curtis is a fellow at Florida Tech's Institute for Cross Cultural Management, and he teaches MBA courses in leadership and people management for the Jack Welch Management Institute.

His training focuses on global leadership, communicating across cultures, managing conflict, leading global teams, and organizational change. He also provides coaching for global leaders, has spearheaded the development of more than 200 courses and workshops, speaks Spanish (has taught more than 50 leadership workshops in Spanish), Portuguese (has facilitated several programs) and French. He has facilitated leadership development programs in North America, Europe, Asia, the Caribbean, and Latin America.

Dr. Curry served as director, World Trade Institute of the Americas and director, Entrena Honduras/Nicaragua. He is a member of the Worldwide Association of Business Coaches, ATD, SHRM (served as a Global Expertise Panelist 2016 and 2017), and the Society for Intercultural Education, Training and Research (SIETAR).

To reach Dr. Curtis D. Curry for information on organizational citizenship behavior, cross-cultural competence, or leadership development, please visit his **website:** globalqli.com or **e-mail:** curtis@globalqli.com

Ensuring Prosperous Knowledge Flow from the Silent Generation Through Generation Z in a Global Workforce

Dr. Cynthia J. Young

Workplaces have an organizational culture that will either support an organization in its pursuit of success or will undermine its worth and ultimately fail. There are currently five generations of employees comprising the workforce throughout the world from the Silent Generation through Generation Z. The different generations must employ purposeful communication to prevent loss of tacit and explicit knowledge within their respective organizations. As I have advanced from the enlisted to the officer ranks in the U.S. Navy to becoming a Department of Defense (DoD) contractor, I continue to work with many of these generations over two decades.

In the military, service members transition from job to job every couple of years. Before moving on to the next job, service members must ensure they transfer the tacit and explicit knowledge to their team so the missions are able to continue progressing as required. There was no holding back of the tacit or explicit knowledge since part of the military culture is to never be the senior person with a secret. In other words, ensure the team has the information needed to avoid being the only person that has the necessary knowledge for the situation. Holding back knowledge of a process from a shipmate would be detrimental to the organization. Sharing knowledge to have that prosperous knowledge flow benefits the team and the individual. During a tour overseas in Bahrain, daily collaboration with other commands located in the United States and underway in the Arabian Gulf, knowledge sharing and knowledge transfer were critical requirements for mission accomplishment.

While organizations have workforces with varying degrees of knowledge and experiences, the culture should support an open learning environment. Storytelling can lead to trust (Al-Qadhi, Nor, Ologbo, & Knight, 2015), which can lead to collaboration. Communications between people at the slow pace of face-to-face communications or letter writing are changing at a quicker pace through computer-mediated communication (Venter, 2017). According to Venter (2017), the Baby Boomer generation primarily communicates using face-to-face communication whereas the first generation who primarily communicates using digital communications is Generation Y (Singh & Dangmei 2016).

Ensuring Prosperous Knowledge Flow from the Silent Generation Through Generation Z in a Global Workforce

Organizational knowledge management is complex on its own, but adding generational differences compounds the issue. Explicit knowledge and tacit knowledge are two categories of knowledge. Explicit knowledge is knowledge shared through formal and systematic processes (Nonaka, Yoyama, & Konno, 2000) or even specific to an industry (Gilson, Lim, Luciano, & Choi, 2013). Tacit knowledge is practical knowledge gained through personal experience, skills, and know-how not known through written guidance (Benson, 2019). Through a comprehensive literature review of generational workplace differences, Jones, Murray, and Tapp (2018) found demographic studies identified employees spanning from the Silent Generation through Generation Z occupy the current workplace.

Knowledge sharing and knowledge transfer must occur within an organization to ensure organizational success (Nonaka, 1994). In simple terms, knowledge sharing occurs based on the willingness of employees to share both explicit and tacit knowledge thereby increasing an organization's competitive advantage (Wang & Wang, 2012). Within an organization, knowledge transfer supports innovation and workforce bonding through the common activities (Martelo-Landroguez & Cegarra-Navarro, 2014; Sankowska, 2013). Based on a case study of knowledge transfer between Baby Boomers and Generation X aerospace engineers, Bethune (2018) recommended that organizations create knowledge sharing activities as a method of building relationships between generations which can provide opportunities for collaboration with an organization facilitating stronger communications and knowledge transfer and retention.

Corporate knowledge sharing primarily occurs through employee communication (Young, 2016). When organizations lack continuity of knowledge flow, the lack of knowledge flow affects an organization's ability to attain or maintain positive performance (Young, 2016). Adding the different behaviors exhibited when generations communicate with each other in a global workforce, an organization may incur additional risks when supporting its customers. With organizational knowledge management supporting prosperity of organizations, and a geographically dispersed workforce challenged by generational communication and cultural differences, organizations need to implement knowledge management practices that address the boundaries of generational gaps and geographic constraints.

Definitions of a cultural workforce can differ when viewed through an organizational culture lens as opposed to a generational culture lens whereas management views organizational culture as a team of similar traits with a shared vision and commitment (Karyotakis & Moustakis, 2016). Employees viewpoint of generational culture differs between age groupings (Karyotakis & Moustakis, 2016). Knowledge flow from the C-suite down to the newest intern and back up to the C-suite must exist for an organization to have a chance to be prosperous. There is a positive correlation between knowledge management practices, such as knowledge sharing and knowledge transfer having a positive impact on firm performance (Lopez-Nicolas & Merono-Cerdan, 2011; Young, 2016). There is also a positive correlation with knowledge management when used in combination with innovation on firm performance (Young, 2016).

Organizations should not view prosperity based only on a dollar amount, but as much as competitive success or growth within the industry to include working with teaming partners. A prosperous knowledge flow could be as simple as learning from the team and gaining knowledge, which, if utilized, could bring about beneficial improvements of the business. Ensuring a prosperous knowledge flow could be as complicated as coordinating and collaborating on a multinational project with a multigenerational team requiring training to baseline the team resulting in professional growth and retention of the entire workforce.

An example of team success through prosperous knowledge flow are drivers using Global Positioning System (GPS) devices. The drivers are using the same picture and the same directions to get from one location to another. The collaboration of knowledge and technology to achieve a goal of arrival at a new location occurs. Like driving to a location using GPS, in an organization with multiple generations of workers, what is important is that the workforce culture ensures knowledge management is a primary role as part of their dynamic capabilities framework (Schneckenberg, Truong, & Mazloomi, 2015).

Generational Identification of a Workforce

Generations are based on ranges of birth years or major events occurring during that generation, but there may be slight variances of the years (Kicheva, 2017). The Silent Generation, also called Veterans or Traditionalists, spans 1925–1945 (Sanner-Stiehr & Vandermause, 2017). Legas and Sims (2011) and Rothman (2016) defined the approximate generational ranges of Baby Boomers as ~1946–1964 and Generation X as ~1965–1980. Rothman (2016) defined Generation Y as 1981–1995. Singh and Dangmei (2016) identified Generation Z as the generation born in the later 1990s who are becoming part of the newest addition to the workforce in the 2000s.

Although there are five generations noted above, Bejikovsky (2016) examined Czech corporations citing that there are only four generations working with the Silent Generation based on the Czech current labor market. The differences noted between the remaining four generations were (a) recruit and development of teams; (b) ability to deal with change; (c) provide motivation, stimulation, and management of employees; and (d) boost productivity, effectiveness of service, and increase competitiveness (Bejikovsky, 2016). The focus of this chapter will remain on the five generations of the workforce noted earlier and will address generational cultural workforce differences, generational communication methods, and global knowledge management challenges as they affect prosperous knowledge flow of a global organization.

Generational Cultural Workforce Differences

Generational cultural workforce differences exist on many levels. Three of the key generational differences are longevity within an organization (Angeline, 2011; Sanner-Stiehr & Vandermause, 2017), employee ownership (O'Boyle, Patel, & Gonzalez-Mule, 2016), and advances in technology (Kicheva, 2017). Independently, these generational differences are important to note as they address different aspects of an organizational culture. When management recognizes these three workforce differences and address them together to support strengthening knowledge flow within an organization, they can create a powerful, synergistic team. One impression when employees start with an organization is that there is a generational gap in longevity of employees within an organization (Angeline, 2011). What is meant is that the Silent Generation and Baby Boomers tend to work extensively for single employers moving vertically within an organization seeking stability, whereas the later generations are used to moving in multiple directions while working through multiple employers to seek growth in their professional goals (Sanner-Stiehr & Vandermause, 2017). An unintended consequence of the later, or younger, generations in seeking professional growth through multiple employers is that they do not get the benefit of gaining knowledge through experiencing the full lifecycle of a project or a program.

By contrast, an unintended consequence of the older generations and their extensive longevity with one or two employers is that they may not gain as much knowledge or learn different aspects of a project or program. Longevity of older generations as opposed to the brevity of younger generations in the workplace may separate the workforce and the culture of the organization and may divide the generations with one group doing things one way and the other group doing things another way, possibly causing conflict in the organization goals of the C-suite. Contributing to the conflict, cross-generational teams may be less production resulting in alienation of employee groups or causing tense working environments when blame results from failed expectations (Angeline, 2011).

A second difference in workforce culture is the use of an Employee Stock Ownership Plan (ESOP) have a more positive, statistically significant relationship to firm performance (O'Boyle,

Patel, & Gonzalez-Mule, 2016). Employee ownership in a company with an ESOP is by fiduciary rights, employee-owned. The culture of employee ownership can be prosperous because an employee-owned company has a company where every employee has a direct impact on the profit or loss of a company. With an ESOP company, qualified employees earn stock in the company that grows with the length of time the employee is with the organization and the salary of the employee. Since ESOP benefits are better for qualified employees who stay with the company longer, there may be a tendency for the older generations to have more stock more stock than the younger generations since older generations are more stable than the younger generations (Angeline, 2011; Sanner-Stiehr & Vandermause, 2017). Remembering that younger generations tend to not stay for as many years with an organization as the older generations do, the overall ownership in the success of the organization may be weaker.

The third difference to note is the use of technology differs between generations. Going beyond the age differences of the generations, understanding the differences between generational experiences, communication methods, and knowledge management practices may lead to ensuring prosperity within an organization and is especially important to knowledge within a developing world (Kicheva, 2017). Generational experiences in technology are one of the easiest to comprehend is the transition from touchtone phones to Smart phones and typewriters to laptop computers and tablets. With the technological advances, knowledge management practices shifted throughout the generations and the industries not to mention influence the organizational culture of a company's workforce.

While the three differences noted are not the only differences a multigenerational workforce will experience, having an organizational culture for businesses which operate out of more than one office or more than one country is challenging. Organizational management needs to address and acknowledge these differences as high importance to ensuring a prosperous knowledge flow. In addition to the third difference, technology, the organizational culture must include varying methods of communication since the different generations utilize varying methods of communication within the workplace (Bidian & McGill, 2018).

Generational Communication Methods

An obvious detriment to communication is linguistic differences, especially in a global workforce in which the host language in one country may be different from another country's host language. With basic language, there is slang used based on the generation of the speaker or of the organization's industry. Either of these may be a perceived barrier that management must overcome to support effective knowledge sharing and knowledge transfer. Al-Qadhi et al. (2015) found that among several differences, languages could affect knowledge sharing in a multinational organization, but at different levels.

Different generational cohorts may keep communication, and inherent with that, tacit knowledge, within the confines of their own generation. Bidian and McGill (2018) conducted a study examining methods of communication between Millennials, Generation X, and Baby Boomers and determined there were no intergenerational differences for sharing knowledge, only some minor proficiency differences in use E-mail, website usage, and video-conferencing, to name a few. A study of Generation Y participants from the hotel industry resulted in a finding that communication patterns between Generation Y and those not part of Generation Y highly influenced Generation Y's understanding of work in the hotel industry (Lewis, 2015). An important tie between these studies to recognize is that knowledge sharing must occur or loss of knowledge will occur when employees depart their respective organizations (Young, 2016). A key method of communication used to transfer knowledge between the varying generations is storytelling. Defined as an easy and relatable method of transferring tacit knowledge of experiences, storytelling supports verbal information sharing (Bethune, 2018), but people can use tacit knowledge to explain experiences when working with explicit knowledge as well (Young, 2016). Storytelling is a method of sharing information, which can be more relaxed and even jovial than a formal knowledge sharing session reaching a cross-cultural and organizationally diverse audience (Barker & Gower, 2010).

Social media supports facilitation of management and externalization of organizational and personal knowledge (Razmara, Kirchner, & Nielsen, 2016). As of 2015, social media was the tool most commonly used by business professionals 21–50 years old (Cardon & Marshall, 2015). Cardon and Marshall (2015) determined through a survey of 227 business professionals that traditional communications the most effective method of team communications over social media although e-mail was the most frequently used method of communication for all participants. Artiz, Walker, and Cardon (2017) reinforced the most effective method that finding through a study of coordination with virtual teams where the teams identified rich channels of social media more useful in team coordination than file sharing, email, web conferencing, messaging, or calling.

Global Knowledge Management Challenges

Knowledge management is a challenge when there are employees or teams physically located in the same office space, but the challenge grows when there are physical boundaries, time zones, or a division of on-site vs. remote employees. There are also different methods of communication such as using social media, video teleconferences, voice-only conference calls, e-mail, or chat potentially in use for collaboration purposes (Jimenez, Boehe, Taras, & Caprar, 2017). Knowledge sharing through social network sites across the enterprise of an organization supports the relationships and interactions of employees, which strengthen an organization (Ellison, Gibbs, & Weber, 2015).

The use of social media requires employees to be knowledgeable in the functions of it and the benefits of it for the customers as well as the organizations that rely on it. Social networking is the primary method for team communication for Generations X and Y to support customer communication (Cardon & Marshall, 2015). A challenge in customer interaction for employees is that the Baby Boomers, and assuming the Silent Generation due to being born earlier than the Baby Boomers, face-to-face communication more so than computer-based communication of Generation Y (Venter, 2017).

Distributed multinational organizations use enterprise social network technology to support knowledge sharing between teams that can be critical to ensuring knowledge sharing occurs throughout the organization to include locations in different time zones (Ellison et al., 2015). Time zones represent challenges in knowledge management that organizations, especially those with offices worldwide, must strive to overcome. The military operates based on Zulu, or Greenwich Mean Time, in their official message traffic correspondence. Using one time zone as a base for message traffic allows all commands who receive operational tasking to avoid calculating the mental math each instance of message traffic while synchronizing operations since they continue to operate in the same time zone.

Collaboration between individuals or teams in a global operation requires planning and forethought. Schneckenberg, Truong, and Mazloomi (2015) determined organizational leaders need to invest in a collaborative technology technological platform to support integration of tacit and explicit knowledge. This functionality can support single structure organizations or glob-ally-dispersed organizations. However, when an organization has global presence with differing levels of the understanding and usage of collaborative technology, there must be an ability and willingness between the workforce, on-site or remote, to collab-orate and overcome these differences in know-how (Cummings, 2004; Razmerita, Kirchner, & Nielsen, 2016). Collaborative tools allow, for good or for bad, organizations to work around the clock to complete work.

Recommendations

Employee communication supports a great deal of corporate knowledge sharing throughout organizations (Young, 2016). Al-Qadhi et al. (2015) determined trust was a critical factor influ-encing knowledge sharing among the workforce and within a multinational environment. Cox and Blake (1991) cited a model of management of cultural diversity that included the need to pro-mote knowledge and acceptance as a management activity within an organization as well as valuing the differences and supporting multinational cultural inclusion. The organization could replicate value of knowledge as part of a multigenerational cultural model as support creation of an inter-unit organization using replication structure to prevent knowledge loss (Kim & Anand, 2018).

In addition to the issues discussed earlier in this chapter, there are other conceivable options to support cultural growth and understanding for consideration. Bowman, Denson, and Park (2016) recommended racial / cultural awareness workshops. Jyoti and Kour's (2015) study assessing cultural intelligence and task performance found the importance cultural intelligence could bring to overall task performance when a person of another nationality performs tasks because it can be acceptance of differ-ences. Knowledge management may be as easy as using intuitive collaborative tools the entire workforce within a dispersed organization can use.

Conclusion

Researchers studied multigeneration management of the workforce for many years and will most assured continue to be studies as future generations of workers find employment and purpose in their lifetimes. Organizational leadership will need to continue knowledge sharing and knowledge transfer within their organizations to maintain the continuity of knowledge flow as they continue to populate around the globe. There will continue to be multiple generations of workers collaborating and the C-suite needs to continue to have the tools and the know-how to address a multigenerational workforce.

Whether the organization is one location with remote workers or an international organization with multiple locations throughout the world, organizations need to have a plan in place to execute and complete their organizational tasking and support their customers without negative impacting the organization's profit/loss statement. Culture is unwieldy, but adding a global workforce aspect, comprised of the various generations in the current workforce, makes it all more of a challenge.

Organizations with a multigenerational workforce should take advantage of the collaborative technology available, but also endear trust between employees through knowledge sharing and active listening. Using the knowledge sharing and knowledge transfer methodologies in support of establishment of an organizational culture to meet organizational and customer objectives is an organizational strength worth pursuing. Through generational identification of a workforce, workforce differences, and concerted efforts to use knowledge management to support prosperity of an organization, the refractive thinker positively supports the organizational culture.

THOUGHTS FROM THE ACADEMIC ENTREPRENEUR

The problem to be solved:

- Ensuring knowledge flow is not hindered due to varying generational cultural differences

The goals:

- Plan success for an organization through tacit and explicit knowledge sharing and knowledge transfer between generations.

The questions to ask:

- How can an organization use generational knowledge to improve workforce culture?

- What tools are available to share tacit and explicit knowledge that can work across generations in the workplace?

Today's Business Application:

- Proactive leaders and managers should respect and work with cultural difference with a multigenerational workforce.

- Plan for an organization culture to include a multigenerational workforce with varying, yet valuable experience and knowledge.

- Ensure knowledge sharing and knowledge flow to allow for flexibility throughout your organizational team.

REFERENCES

Al-Qadhi, Y. H., Nor, K. M., Ologbo, A. C., & Knight, M. B. (2015). Knowledge sharing in a multi-nationality workforce: Examining the factors that influence knowledge sharing among employees of diverse nationalities. *Human Systems Management, 34,* 149–165. doi:10.3233/HSM-150844

Angeline, T. (2011). Managing generational diversity at the workplace: Expectations and perceptions of different generations of employees. *African Journal of Business Management, 5*(2), 249–244. doi:10.5897/AJBM10.335

Appelbaum, S. H., Benyo, C., Gunkel, H., Ramadan, S., Sakkal, F., & Wolff, D. (2012). Transferring corporate knowledge via succession planning: Analysis and solutions–Part 2. *Industrial and Commercial Training, 44,* 379–388. doi:10.1108/00197851211267956

Artiz, J., Walker, R., & Cardon, P. W. (2017). Media use in virtual teams of varying levels of coordination. *Business and Professional Communication Quarterly, 81*(2), 222–243. doi:10.1177/2329490617723114

Barker, R. T., & Gower, K. (2010). Strategic application of storytelling in organizations: Toward effective communication in a diverse world. *Journal of Business Communication, 47*(3), 295–312. doi:10.1177/0021943610369782

Bejtkowsky, J. (2016). The employees of Baby Boomers generation, Generation X, Generation Y, and Generation Z in selected Czech corporations as conceivers of development and competitiveness in their corporation. *Journal of Competitiveness, 8*(4), 105–112. doi:10.7441/joc.2016.04.07

Benson, J. (2019). Deliberative democracy and the problem of tacit knowledge. *Politics, Philosophy, and Economics, 18*(1), 76–97. doi:10.1177/1470594X18782086

Bethune, M. (2018). *Save that thought: A case study of how knowledge is transferred between Baby Boomers and Generation-X aerospace engineers* (Doctoral dissertation). Available from ProQuest Dissertations and Theses database. (UMI No. 10828846)

Bidian, C., & Evans, M. M. (2018). Examining inter-generational knowledge sharing and technological preferences. *European Conference on Knowledge Management,* 95-XVI. Retrieved from https://www.academia.edu/37597057/Examining_Inter-Generational_Knowledge_Sharing_and_Technological_Preferences

Bowman, N. A., Denson, N., & Park, J. J. (2016). Racial/cultural awareness workshops and post-college civic engagement: A propensity score matching approach. *American Educational Research Journal, 53,* 1556–1587. doi:10.3102/0002831216670510

Cardon, P. W., & Marshall, B. (2015). The hype and reality of social media use for work collaboration and team communication. *International Journal of Business Communication, 52*(3), 273–293. doi:10.1177/23294888414525446

Cavaliere, V., & Lombardi, S. (2015). Exploring different cultural configurations: How do they affect subsidiaries' knowledge sharing behaviors? *Journal of Knowledge Management, 19*(2), 144–163. doi:10.1108/JKM-04-2014-0167

Chang, C. L., & Lin, T. (2015). The role of organizational culture in the knowledge management process. *Journal of Knowledge Management, 19,* 433–455. doi:10.1108/JKM-08-2014-0353

Cox, T. H., & Blake, S. (1991). Managing cultural diversity: Implications for organization competitiveness. *Academy of Management Executive, 5*(3), 45–56. Retrieved from http://www.jstor.org/stable/4165021

Cummings, J. N. (2004). Work groups, structural diversity, and knowledge sharing in a global organization. *Management Science, 50,* 352–364. doi:10.1287/mnsc.1030.0134

Ellison, N. B., Gibbs, J. L., & Weber, M. S. (2015). The use of enterprise social network sites for knowledge sharing in distributed organizations: The role of organizational affordances. *American Behavioral Scientist, 59*(1), 103–123. doi:10.1177/0002764214540510

Gilson, L. L., Lim, H. S., Luciano, M. M., & Choi, J. N. (2013). Unpacking the cross-level effects of tenure diversity, explicit knowledge, and knowledge sharing on individual creativity. *Journal of Occupational & Organizational Psychology, 86,* 203–222. doi:10.1111/joop.12011

Holten, A-L. Hancock, G. R., Persson, R. Hansen, A. M., & Hogh, A. (2016). Knowledge hoarding: Antecedent or consequent of negative acts? The mediating role of trust and justice. *Journal of Knowledge Management, 20*(2), 215–229. doi:10.1108/JKM-06-2015-0222

Jha, B., & Kumar, A. (2016). Employee engagement: A strategic tool to enhance performance. *DAWN: Journal for Contemporary Research in Management, 3*(2), 21–29. Retrieved from http://www.psgim.ac.in/journals/index.php/jcrm

Jimenez, A., Boehe, D. M., Taras, V., & Caprar, D. V. (2017). Working across boundaries: Current and future perspectives on global virtual teams. *Journal of International Management, 23,* 341–349. doi:10.1016/j.intman.2017.05.001

Jones, J. S., Murray, S. R., & Tapp, S. R. (2018). Generational differences in the workplace. *Journal of Business Diversity, 18*(2), 88–97. doi:10.33423/jbd.v18i2

Jyoti, J., & Kour, S. (2015). Assessing the cultural intelligence and task performance equation: Mediating role of cultural adjustment. *Cross Cultural Management: An International Journal, 22*(2), 235–258. doi:10.1108/CCM-04-2013-0072

Karyotakis, K. M., & Moustakis, V. S. (2015). Organizational factors, organizational culture, job satisfaction, and entrepreneurial orientation in public administration. *The European Journal of Applied Economics, 13*(1), 47–59. doi:10.5937/ejae13-10781

Kicheva, T. (2017). Management of employees from different generations—Challenge for Bulgarian manages and HR professionals. *Economic Alternatives, 1,*

103–121. Retrieved from https://www.unwe.bg/uploads/Alternatives/Kicheva_ea_en_br_1_2017.pdf

Kim, S., & Anand, J. (2018). Knowledge complexity and the performance of inter-unit knowledge replication structures. *Strategic Management Journal, 39,* 1959–1989. doi:10.1002/smj2899

Legas, M., & Sims, C. (2011). Leveraging generational diversity in today's workplace. *Online Journal for Workforce Education and Development, 5*(3), 1–9. Retrieved from http://opensiuc.lib.siu.edu

Lewis, R. A. (2015). Generation Y at work: Insight from experiences in the hotel sector. *International Journal of Business and Management, 3*(1), 1–17. doi:10.20472/BM.2015.3.1.001

Li, X. (2013). The impact of job engagement on tacit knowledge transfer. *International Business and Management, 6,* 115–120. doi:10.3968/j.ibm.1923842820130602.1130

López-Nicolás, C, & Meroño-Cerdán, Á. L. (2011). Strategic knowledge management, innovation, and performance. *International Journal of Information Management, 31,* 502–509. doi:10.1016/j.ijinfomgt.2011.02.003

Martelo-Landroguez, S., & Cegarra-Navarro, J. G. (2014). Linking knowledge corridors to customer value through knowledge processes. *Journal of Knowledge Management, 18,* 342–365. doi:10.1108/JKM-07–2013–0284

Nonaka, I. (1994). A dynamic theory of organizational knowledge creation. *Organization Science, 5,* 14–37. Retrieved from http://orgsci.journal.informs.org

Nonaka, I., Toyama, R., & Konno, N. (2000). SECI, *ba,* and leadership: A unified model of dynamic knowledge creation. *Long Range Planning, 33,* 5–34. Retrieved from http://www.elsevier.com/locate/lrp

O'Boyle, E. H., Patel, P. C., & Gonzalez-Mule, E. (2016). Employee ownership and firm performance: A meta-analysis. *Human Resource Management Journal, 26,* 425–448. doi:10.1111/1748–8583.12115

Razmerita, L., Kirchner, K., & Nielsen, P. (2016). What factors influence knowledge management sharing in organizations? A social dilemma perspective of social media communication. *Journal of Knowledge Management, 20,* 1225–1246. doi:10.1108/JKM-03–2016–0112

Rothman, D. (2016). A tsunami of learners called Generation Z. Retrieved from http://mdle.net/Journal/A_Tsunami_of_Learners_Called_Generation_Z.pdf

Sankowska, A. (2013). Relationships between organizational trust, knowledge transfer, knowledge creation, and firm's innovativeness. *Learning Organization, 20,* 85–100. doi:10.1108/09696471311288546

Sanner-Stiehr, E., & Vandermause, R. K. (2017). Can't we all just get along? A dual-theory approach to understanding and managing the multigenerational workplace. *Journal of Organizational Psychology, 17*(2), 103–110. doi:10.33423/jop.v17i2.1687

Schneckenberg, D., Truong, Y., & Mazloomi, H. (2015). Microfoundations of innovative capabilities: The leverage of collaborative technologies on organizational learning and knowledge management in a multinational corporation. *Technological Forecasting and Social Change, 100,* 356–368 doi:10.1016/j.techfore.2015.08.008

Singh, A. P., & Dangmei, J. (2016). Understanding the Generation Z: The future workforce. *South-Asian Journal of Multidisciplinary Studies, 3*(3), 1–5. Retrieved from http://sajms.com/volume-3-issue-3/understanding-generation-z-future-workforce/

Venkitachalam, K., & Busch, P. (2012). Tacit knowledge: Review and possible research directions. *Journal of Knowledge Management, 16,* 357–372. doi:10.1108/13673271211218915

Venter, E. (2017). Bridging the communication gap between Generation Y and the Baby Boomer generation. *International Journal of Adolescence and Youth, 22,* 497–507. doi:10.1080/02673843.2016.1267022

Wang, Z., & Wang, N. (2012). Knowledge sharing, innovation, and firm performance. *Expert Systems with Applications, 39,* 8899–8908. doi:10.1016/j.eswa.2012.02.017

Whyte, G., & Classen, S. (2012). Using storytelling to elicit tacit knowledge from SMEs. *Journal of Knowledge Management, 16,* 950–962. doi:10.1108/13673271211276218

Wijetunge, P. (2012). Organizational storytelling as a method of tacit-knowledge transfer: Case study from a Sri Lankan university. *International Information and Library Review, 44,* 212–223. doi:10.1016/j.iilr.2012.09.001

Young, C. J. (2016). *Knowledge management and innovation on firm performance of United States ship repair* (Doctoral dissertation). Available from ProQuest Dissertations and Theses database. (UMI No. 10042541)

About the Author . . .

Dr. Cynthia J. Young resides in Chesapeake, Virginia. Dr. Cindy holds several accredited degrees; a Bachelor of Arts (BA) in English Language and Literature from the University of Maryland, College Park; two Masters of Business Administration (MBA), one in e-commerce and one in advanced management studies, from Trident University International; and a Doctor of Business Administration (DBA) in Project Management from Walden University.

Dr. Cindy is a Tomahawk Planning System Curriculum Developer and Instructor with Leidos, a defense contracting company, after retiring as a Surface Warfare Officer with 23 years in the U.S. Navy. She is a past-Chair of American Society for Quality, Tidewater, Section 1128, and a member of the Project Management Institute, Golden Key International Honor Society, and Delta Mu Delta International Business Honor Society.

Dr. Cindy holds professional certifications as a Project Management Professional, a Lean Six Sigma Master Black Belt, and as an ASQ-Certified Manager of Quality / Organizational Excellence. Her doctoral study, *Knowledge Management and Innovation on Firm Performance of United States Ship Repair,* provided her the opportunity to gain additional professional and academic expertise to facilitate improvements in organizational knowledge management. She is also the author of *Chapter 3: Using Leadership to Improve Firm Performance Through Knowledge Management* from *The Refractive Thinker: Volume XI: Women in Leadership.*

To reach Dr. Cynthia J. Young for information on refractive thinking or guest speaking, please visit her on **LinkedIn:** https://www.linkedin.com/in/drcindyyoung/ or **e-mail:** drcynthiajyoung@gmail.com

CHAPTER 5

Escaping the Cultural Psychic Prison—Employee Engagement as a Refractive Prism

Dr. Le-Marlié Marais

The goal of this chapter is to convert scholarly findings related to leaders' strategies for effective employee engagement into practical information suitable for practitioners to apply in the organizational context, regardless of the industry type or geographical location. A key focus in this chapter is on how organizational leaders and managers can escape from the cultural psychic prison created through organizational culture, climate, and historical practices. The cultural psychic prison is type of mental model resulting from cultural and organizational expectations, preventing leaders and managers from *seeing* potential solutions that do not fit their existing mental models. The refractive light from the prism that is employee engagement provides leaders and managers with the means to escape their cultural psychic prison. Practitioners should have a deeper understanding of the conditions (Kahn, 1990), facets (Shuck & Reio, 2011), and outcomes associated with employee engagement (Kiliannan& Adjovu, 2015; Rana, 2015), before embarking on organizational investment in employee engagement (Shuck & Rose, 2013; Shuck, Zigarmi, & Owen, 2015; Valentin, 2014). At the end of this chapter, both scholars and practitioners should have a deeper understanding of employee engagement as a construct, possible strategies that leaders could use, and the iterative process required for establishing and maintaining employee engagement.

Employee Engagement in the Organizational Context

Employee engagement, despite many years of research, remains a construct that is difficult to define. Employee engagement is not something that leaders and managers can "demand from employees, artificially create, or inflate at will" (Shuck & Rose, 2013, p. 343). Without engaged employees and regardless of the reason for disengagement, organizations globally experience a decline in organizational productivity, across all types of organizations and industries (Anitha, 2014, Kipfelsberger & Kark, 2018; Shuck & Reio, 2014). In their 2017 study, Gallup found that only 15% of full time employed employees globally reported feeling engaged at work. Marais (2017) argued that some leaders lacked the skills and strategies to engage employees at work. While researchers and practitioners agree that there is no *one-size-fits-all* solution to employee engagement (Fearon, McLaughlin, & Morris, 2013; Townsend, Wilkinson, & Burgess, 2014), there are fundamental principles that organizational leaders and managers must meet to bring about employee engagement, underpinned by the three facets of employee engagement as described by Shuck and Reio (2011). The three facets of employee engagement are cognitive, emotional, and behavioral engagement (Shuck & Reio, 2011), which are easily distinguishable from types of engagement such as work engagement, employee engagement, and organizational engagement (Andrew & Sofian, 2012). From the existing literature and research findings, emerges the business problem *leaders lack the skills and strategies to engage employees.* For this chapter, employee engagement refers to an employee feeling involved in the organization in terms of feeling cognitively, emotionally, and behaviorally engaged in achieving organizational goals (Shuck & Wollard, 2010).

Researchers and practitioners agree that drivers are the aspects that cause engagement (Rees, Alfes, & Gatenby, 2013). Drivers or antecedents of engagement include, among other (a) trust and integrity, (b) the nature of the job, (c) employee development opportunities, (d) growth opportunities, organizational pride, and (f) supervisor-employee relationship (Sahoo & Sahu, 2009). One way to address this lack of skill and understanding is to review the skills and strategies leaders use at organizations that have engaged employees. Most organizations' culture and leadership styles develop over the life of the organization, while some organizational cultures depend on industry culture or individual leadership style. This begs the question, are organizations and their leaders prisoners of their own psychic prisons?

Escaping the Cultural Psychic Prison

Irrespective of the industry, organizational leaders globally experience a continued decline in productivity caused by disengaged employees (Anitha, 2014; Kipfelsberger & Kark, 2018; Osborne & Hammoud, 2017; Shuck & Reio, 2014). Osbourne and Hammoud (2017) identified employee engagement as one of the most significant challenges in the workplace. Morgan (2016) noted that metaphors and metonymy served as a creative and expansive process that played a crucial role in both practice and theory while also constructing much-needed meaning in everyday life. One might consider contextualizing employee engagement and the lack of skills and strategies to engage employees by viewing the constructs through the lens of a psychic prison. The psychic prison is one of Morgan's (2011) eight metaphors proposed for reframing and understanding organizations.

To pin down and articulate the specific metaphorical and

metonymical meaning and details (Morgan, 2016) of the psychic prison, one needs to understand its origin. The psychic prison metaphor uses the imagery created by Plato's allegory of the cave (D'Olimpio, 2019), as discussed between Socrates and Glaucon. The gist of the allegory is that there are several people in a darkened cave. The cave dwellers have been in the cave since early childhood and do not know any world other than their darkened cave. Shackles restrict the cave dwellers' mobility such that they cannot move around nor turn their heads to look around.

As a consequence, the cave dwellers create their world based on the shadows they see against the cave wall and the noises they hear echoing through the cave; they never learn or know more about the origin of the shadows or the noises other than what they observe and discuss between themselves. One of the philosophical questions of the allegory was, if one cave dweller was to be freed one night and showed the truth (i.e., that there are others creating the noises and shadows and that the cave was but a small piece of the bigger world), what would this cave dweller do with this information? If the freed cave dweller returned to the cave, would the others believe his or her version of reality or simply think of it as madness (D'Olimpio, 2019; Morgan, 2011)?

The central idea behind the psychic prison as a metaphor for organizations is that those in the cave know their reality only as they perceive their reality in the confines of the shackles and the cave. They live in blissful ignorance of the part their perceived reality plays in the bigger world, or how knowledge of the bigger world might change their current perceptions. Similarly, organizational climate and culture might become a psychic prison in which organizational leaders and managers operate, specifically, in terms of leader behavior, strategies, and communication within the organization. The psychic prison becomes a trap to which many organizations fall victim. Leaders and managers require a deeper understanding of employee engagement and the strategies and skills needed to bring about employee engagement (Marais, 2017), to better understand the organizational trap posed by the psychic prison and how to escape their psychic prison.

Putting the Pieces Together

From its first accepted mention by Kahn in 1990, researchers disagreed on a single definition for employee engagement as a construct (Keeble-Ramsay & Armitage, 2014). Khan (1990) introduced the needs-satisfying approach inducing that employees will only feel engaged at work through meeting their three psychological conditions (meaningfulness, emotional safety, and availability of resources). Later, Shuck and Reio (2011) identified three facets of engagement, namely cognitive, emotional, and behavioral engagement, in addition to the three conditions or antecedents of engagement. In a 2017 study, Marais drew comparisons between various antecedents identified in employee engagement research and Kahn's conditions for engagement based on research findings. The conditions for engagement (Kahn, 1990) drive the first of the three facets of engagement (Shuck & Herd, 2012; Shuck & Reio, 2011; Shuck & Reio, 2014), as depicted in Figure 1. Importantly, the three facets of engagement are dependent on each other such that "cognitive engagement preceded emotional engagement, which in turn precedes behavioral engagement" (Marais, 2017, p. 36). Employees need a positive appraisal of all three conditions for engagement (Kahn, 1990) for cognitive engagement to occur (Shuck, Twyford, Reio, & Shuck, 2014). For employees to experience emotional engagement (which follows cognitive engagement), they need to express a willingness to invest themselves in their work and organization (Shuck & Rose, 2013). Note that the decision to emotionally engage remains with the employee and shapes behavioral engagement (Shuck & Herd, 2012). Last, leaders or managers can only obtain behavioral engagement (the only visible form of engagement) when employees are willing to and apply discretionary effort (Shuck & Reio, 2011). Many researchers associate behavioral engagement with improved productivity and performance (Alfes, Shantz, Truss, & Soane, 2013; Kiliannan & Adjovu, 2015; Shuck & Herd, 2012; Shuck & Reio, 2014). Additionally, and possibly, more importantly, meeting the conditions *and* facets of engagement result in outcomes that leave employees feeling satisfied and fulfilled (Kaliannan & Adjovu, 2015).

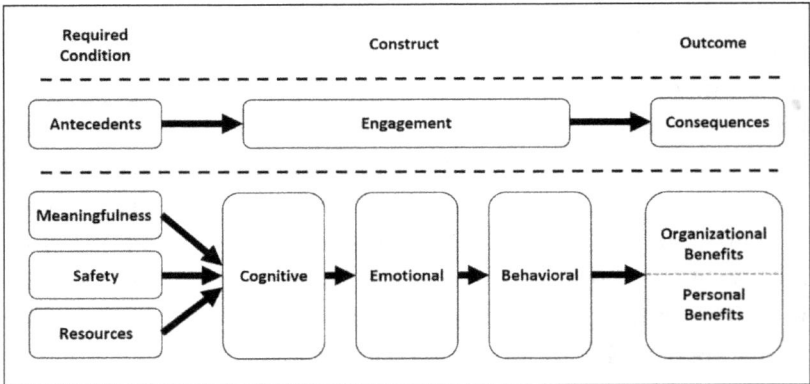

Figure 1. Conceptual model of employee engagement as a process.

Organizational leaders and managers must not approach employee engagement as a single, once-off action (Keeble-Ramsay & Armitage, 2014); instead, employee engagement requires organizational commitment throughout the organization starting at the highest level over the life of the organization (Keeble-Ramsay & Armitage, 2014; Shuck & Herd, 2012). Organizational leaders and managers might create an environment conducive for engagement by focusing on social exchange theory and building on reciprocity between individuals (Jose & Mampilly, 2012; Rees, Alfes, & Gatenby, 2013; Shuck et al., 2014). Employees who experienced and perceived their organization as supportive felt obligated to reciprocate by engaging (Rothmann & Welsch, 2013). Conversely, engagement occurs on a continuum ranging from actively engaged, to unengaged, and lastly, disengaged (Griffiths & Karanika-Murray, 2012; Kumar & Sia, 2012; Valentin, 2014). Finally, organizational leaders and managers should be aware of the unintended consequences of over-engagement; employees may have difficulty balancing voluntary over-involvement at work and their private lives (Karatepe, 2013; Valentin, 2014). When experiencing over-engagement, sometimes referred to as *workaholism,* compulsion and obsession drive employees, whereas, in active engagement, intrinsic motivators drive employees (Shimazu, Shaufeli, Kubota, & Kawakami, 2012).

Strategies for Employee Engagement

Emergent from the findings of Marais' (2017) single case study that explored the strategies and skills mining leaders used to engage employees are that leader behavior, situationally relevant strategies, and focused communication improved employee engagement. The central research question of the study was what strategies do South African mining leaders use to engage employees? Marais collected data by using an interview protocol for leaders and followers, respectively. The leader interviews were semistructured, face-to-face interviews with four mining leaders, while the employee interview was a focus group consisting of nine employees. Shuck and Reio's (2011) engagement framework served as the theory that provided the conceptual framework for the study. The eligibility criteria for participant selection were that eligible participants had at least one direct report, possessed at least two years of experience with employee engagement, and represented different leadership levels in the organization (equivalent to hierarchical levels in traditional organizations).

Marais purposively identified participants from a group of 150 employees at a gold mining company in South Africa. The relatively small sample size aligned with qualitative research practices where the focus is not on the generalizability of the research findings but instead on gaining an in-depth understanding of the phenomenon. Following data collection and organization, Marais used methodological triangulation to analyze interview and focus group data collected, identifying and tagging meaningful units with appropriate labels that emerged from the data. For documentary data, Marais used content analysis and codes to identify emergent themes.

Before reviewing these emergent strategies and skills in detail, it is essential to relate *what is known* to *what can be done*. Enter employee engagement as a refractive prism. A dispersive or refractive prism allows for the separation of "white light into its constituent spectral colors" (Esfahlani, Karkar, Lissek, & Mosig, 2016, p. 1). I propose that organizational leaders and managers use employee engagement as a refractive prism, implementing strategies and skills to engage employees by refracting the white light into its constituent colors within the organization. In this instance, Plato's allegory of the cave (D'Olimpio, 2019) represents the organization, and using the refractive prism allows organizational leaders to break free from the psychic prison. Similarly, the psychic prison represents the organization *imprisoned* by the historical and current cultural restrictions, governed by the cave dwellers' perceived reality, while implementing employee engagement represents the organization's escape from this psychic prison.

Leader Behavior Improved Employee Engagement

One of the three themes that emerged from the Marais (2017) study was that leader behavior improved employee engagement.

Interestingly, leader behavior in this context consisted of three subthemes namely (a) the quality of interaction between leader and follower, (b) competency of the leader, and (c) creating an environment conducive to engagement. Face-to-face leader interviews and focus group discussions indicated that leaders and followers perceived these three leader behaviors as intertwined and interconnected.

Personal interaction with employees, the ability to create a participative environment for employees, and the ability to create understanding among employees drove the quality of interaction theme. Specific leader behaviors highlighted by leaders and followers included leaders that (a) showed a personal interest in employees; (b) allowed them to participate in problem-solving, (c) helped employees understand the requirements of the work environment; (d) clarified information shared to contribute to achieving a common organizational goal; and (e) displayed consistent, fair, and approachable behavior. These specific behaviors underpinning the quality of interaction and its three subthemes are by no means an exhaustive list and would likely be unique to each organization; in the Marais (2017) study, these emerged as the most prominent behaviors.

The next significant leader behavior that emerged from the data is that the competence of leaders was essential to employee engagement (Marais, 2017). The underpinning subthemes of leading from the front, leaders' ability, and showing and telling underpinned the leader competence theme. Leader behavior that personifies leading from the front is leaders' ability to be an example for and give guidance to their followers. Furthermore, from the interviews emerged that leaders incapable of performing tasks they expected their direct reports to perform, decreased engagement. All participants agreed that it was more than reasonable to expect leaders to demonstrate their ability through the act of leading. The importance of the act of leading further emerged through the concept of using a *show and tell* approach. The show and tell approach meant leaders were able to demonstrate what they expected of followers by showing followers how to execute the task, a form of on-the-job training. Additionally, leaders believed (and employees confirmed) that demonstrating experience through the action of leading improved engagement (Marais, 2017).

The third significant leader behavior that improved engagement was the creation of an environment conducive to employee engagement. Participants agreed that leaders needed to demonstrate specific behaviors to create engagement-conducive environments. These behaviors are (a) building trust relationships with employees and (b) the facilitation of sharing a common goal. Importantly, these two behaviors or actions were co-dependent and interdependent; meaning one could not exist without the other. Followers believed that the leader's responsibility was to create an environment in which employees felt safe and engaged. Employees further believed that when there was a trust relationship, they were more likely to execute decisions than question them. Furthermore, findings indicated that part of the trust relationship was clarity about role expectations and responsibilities, and the confidence to address sensitive personal issues that might impact on work performance. As an extension of the discussion of building trust between leader and followers, participants noted that the need exists for a common goal; there could be only one goal free of confusion and ambiguity if there was an existing trust relationship between leaders and followers. Participants noted that when there was a well-defined, common goal, they felt a sense of belonging and confidence in the future of the organization.

Situationally Relevant Strategies Improve Employee Engagement

The second significant finding and theme that emerged from Marais' (2017) study was that situationally relevant strategies improved employee engagement. Leaders and participants stressed the importance of considering the situational context when formulating strategies for engagement (Marais, 2017). Additionally, participants confirmed that there was no *one-size-fits-all* employee engagement strategy (Marais, 2017). Key concepts that emerged from the interviews and focus group was that engagement strategies needed to

- Account for individual employee needs

- Address specific situations (such as dealing with sufficing) that resulted in disengagement

- Acknowledge and recognize employee contributions to achieving organizational goals

- Have a sincere and authentic intention (i.e., not exploit employees' commitment to the exclusive benefit of the organization)

- Allow employees to take responsibility and ownership of relevant processes

- Instill a sense of belonging and involvement in employees. (Marais, 2017)

Focused Communication Strategies Improved Employee Engagement

The third finding and theme of Marais' (2017) study was that focused communication improved employee engagement. Interestingly, participants referred to communication and employee engagement in an almost synonymous way, which is indicative of how deeply leaders entrenched communication in their employee engagement strategies (Marais, 2017). Two subthemes, namely, the level of communication and the role of downward communication, emerged as underpinning focused communication (Marais, 2017). Level of communication referred to leaders' ability to word and address their message in such a way that their recipients understood the intended meaning while downward communication referred to leaders ensuring the communication of the same message to all levels within the organization (Marais, 2017). Other specific aspects of communication that participants flagged as affecting employee engagement included

- The use of face-to-face versus written communication and how this affect leaders' ability to express themselves adequately

- Transparency of message and ensuring there were no hidden messages

- Context of the message by creating a shared sense of the meaning

- Message language and intent appropriate to the intended audience

- Interpreting nonverbal cues in two-way communication to prevent misunderstandings. (Marais, 2017)

Iterative 4-stage RACA Process

Notwithstanding the fact that there is no single *one-size-fits-all* employee engagement strategy, leaders and managers must develop an understanding of organizational interactions (Fearon et al., 2013; Townsend et al., 2014) and universal underlying principles for effective engagement strategies (Marais, 2017). First, organizational leaders and managers need to understand that they cannot simply copy employee engagement strategies from another organization because each organization has its own situational indicators and requirements (Marais, 2017). Second, organizational leaders and managers must never fall into the trap of implementing employee engagement strategies to the exclusive benefit of the organization (Marais, 2017). Employees decide to engage at work based on their experience of their work environment by displaying discretionary effort (Gupta & Sharma, 2016). Similarly, Gupta and Sharma (2016) pointed out that employee engagement was a two-way process, requiring organizational investment in employees resulting in employees reciprocating with displaying discretionary effort toward achieving organizational goals. Therefore, any further action should focus on deriving mutual benefit for both the organization and the employee (outcomes as depicted in Figure 1). Organizations benefit from employee engagement through increased organizational performance (productivity and profitability), while effecting positive social change by improving employees' quality of life at work and home, level of satisfaction at work, and employees' level of personal well-being.

Organizational leaders and managers might consider implementing an iterative 4-stage RACA approach consisting of review (R), assessment (A), comparison (C), and adjustment (A). Essentially, organizations would start the process with a review of employee engagement as perceived by leaders and employees in the organization. The purpose of the review is to gain a better understanding of the organizational interactions that may affect employee engagement. Ideally, the review process should focus on existing leader behavior, the relevance of situational employee engagement strategies, and the existing and frequently used communication strategies. Upon completion of the review, leaders and managers should move on to the assessment of current practices in terms of leader behavior, situational appropriateness of strategies, and communication strategies, specifically from the employees' perspective. Employee perception drives the assessment phase because research supports the notion that employees' experience of engagement influences their perception and interpretation of their work environment, and subsequently their decision to actively engage (AbuKhalifeh & Som, 2013; Andrew & Sofian 2012; Keeble-Ramsay & Armitage, 2014; Shuck & Reio, 2013). The third phase of comparison involves comparing employee engagement strategy expectations against the current practice to identify areas for improvement. Organizational leaders and managers should use these areas for improvement to inform the fourth phase of the iterative process—adjustment. Using areas for improvement to guide strategic changes aligning expectations and current practice should form the basis for an organization's formal employee engagement strategy.

Conclusion

By using employee engagement as a refractive prism, organizational leaders escape their cultural psychic prisons. Employee engagement as a refractive prism comes to organizations through strategies that focus on leader behavior, situationally relevant strategies, and focused communication. Using the iterative 4-phase RACA process, leaders can develop employee engagement strategies that meet the three conditions for engagement (meaningfulness, safety, and availability of resources). With the meeting of these three conditions, leaders can work toward achieving the three facets of employee engagement (cognitive, emotional, and behavioral engagement). Leaders will know their strategies are effective when employees freely apply discretionary effort to help organizations achieve their goals. Leaders should periodically repeat the iterative 4-phased RACA process given that engagement is never in a static state as described by Shuck and Rose (2013). Using the iterative 4-phased RACA process allows leaders and managers to engage in refractive thinking–going beyond the constraints of psychic prisons and refractive prisms–through employee engagement. Organizational leaders that can maintain employee engagement in their organizations will experience organizational benefits (improved productivity and profitability) and personal benefits for employees (improved well-being and satisfaction at work).

THOUGHTS FROM THE ACADEMIC ENTREPRENEUR

The problem to be solved:

- Preparing for and managing employee engagement strategies in organizations

The goals:

- Understanding how to improve employee engagement by implementing organization-specific employee engagement strategies.

- Understanding how leaders use employee engagement to create mutually beneficial outcomes for the organization and its employees.

The questions to ask:

- How can organizations effectively implement employee engagement strategies?

- Can self-imposed organizational culture "restrictions" be overcome to create a working environment that is conducive to employee engagement?

Today's Business Application:

- Effective leaders and managers who understand employee engagement and its organizational interactions and acknowledge employees' need for engagement are better equipped to formulate and implement effective employee engagement strategies, regardless of industry type or geographical location.

- Following an iterative process of Review, Assessment, Comparison, and Adjustment (RACA) is fundamental to establish and maintain appropriate employee engagement strategies.

- Continuous communication within the organization will help leaders and managers identify suitable strategies for employee engagement.

REFERENCES

AbuKhalifeh, A., & Som, A. (2013). The antecedents affecting employee engagement and organizational performance. *Asian Social Science, 9*(7), 41–46. doi:10.5539/ass.v9n7p41

Alfes, K., Shantz, A., Truss, C., & Soane, E. (2013). The link between perceived human resource management practices, engagement, and employee behavior: A moderated mediation model. *International Journal of Human Resource Management, 24,* 330–351. doi:10.1080/09585192.2012.679950

Andrew, O. C., & Sofian, S. (2012). Individual factors and work outcomes of employee engagement. *Procedia—Social and Behavioral Sciences, 40,* 498–508. doi:10.1016/j.sbspro.2012.03.222

Anitha, J. (2014). Determinants of employee engagement and their impact on employee performance. *International Journal of Productivity and Performance Management, 63,* 308–323. doi:10.1108/IJPPM-01-2013-0008

D'Olimpio, L. (19 March 2019). Ethics explainer: Plato's Cave. [Online article]. Retrieved from https://ethics.org.au/ethics-explainer-platos-cave/

Esfahlani, H., Karkar, S., Lissek, H., & Mosig, J. (2016). Acoustic dispersive prism. *Scientific Reports, 6,* 1–10. doi:10.1038/srep18911

Fearon, C., McLaughlin, H., & Morris, L. (2013). Conceptualizing work engagement: An individual, collective and organizational efficacy perspective. *European Journal of Training and Development, 37,* 244–256. doi:10.1108/03090591311312723

Griffiths, M., & Karanika-Murray, M. (2012). Contextualizing over-engagement in work: Towards a more global understanding of workaholism as an addiction. *Journal of Behavioral Addictions, 1,* 87–95. doi:10.1556/JBA.1.2012.002

Gupta, N., & Sharma, V. (2016). Exploring employee engagement—A way to better business performance. *Global Business Review, 17,* 45–63. doi:10.1177/0972150916631082

Jose, G., & Mampilly, S. (2012). Satisfaction with HR practices and employee engagement: A social exchange perspective. *Journal of Economics & Behavioral Studies, 4,* 423–430. Retrieved from http://www.ifrnd.org/JournalDetail.aspx?JournalID=2

Kahn, W. A. (1990). Psychological conditions of personal engagement and disengagement at work. *Academy of Management Journal, 33,* 692–725. doi:10.2307/256287

Kaliannan, M., & Adjovu, S. (2015). Effective employee engagement and organizational success: A case study. *Procedia—Social and Behavioral Science, 172,* 161–168. doi:10.1016/j.sbspro.2015.01.350

Karatepe, O. (2013). High-performance work practices and hotel employee performance: The mediation of work engagement. *International Journal of Hospitality Management, 32,* 132–140. doi:10.1016/j.ijhm.2012.05.003

Keeble-Ramsay, D., & Armitage, A. (2014). HRD challenges when faced with disengaged UK workers. *Journal of Workplace Learning, 26,* 217–231. doi:10.1108/JWL-12-2013-0112

Kipfelsberger, P., & Kark, R. (2018). 'Killing me softly with his/her song': How leaders dismantle followers' sense of work meaningfulness. *Frontiers in Psychology, 9,* 1–14. doi:10.3389/fpsyg.2018.00654

Kumar, R., & Sia, S. (2012). Employee engagement: Explicating the contribution of the work environment. *Management and Labour Studies, 37,* 31–43. doi:10.1177/0258042X1103700104

Marais, L. (2017). *Exploring leaders' strategies for employee engagement in the South African mining industry* (Doctoral dissertation). Available from ProQuest Dissertations and Theses database. (UMI No. 10256071)

Morgan, G. (2016). Commentary: Beyond Morgan's eight metaphors. *Human Relations, 69,* 1029–1042. doi:10.1177/0018726715624497

Morgan, G. (2006). *Images of organization.* Thousand Oaks, CA: Sage.

Osborne, S., & Hammoud, M. (2017). Effective employee engagement in the workgroup. International *Journal of Applied Management and Technology, 16,* 50–67. doi:10.5590/IJAMT.2017.16.1.04

Rees, C., Alfes, K., & Gatenby, M. (2013). Employee voice and engagement: Connections and consequences. *International Journal of Human Resource Management, 24,* 2780–2798. doi:10.1080/09585192.2013.763843

Rothmann, S., & Welsh, C. (2013). Employee engagement: The role of psychological conditions. Management Dynamics, 22(1), 14–26. Retrieved from http://www.reference.sabinet.co.za/sa_epublication/mandyn

Shimazu, A., Schaufeli, W., Kubota, K., & Kawakami, N. (2012). Do workaholism and work engagement predict employee well-being and performance in opposite directions? *Industrial Health, 50,* 316–321. doi:10.2486/indhealth.MS1355

Shuck, B., & Herd, A. M. (2012). Employee engagement and leadership: Exploring the convergence of two frameworks and implications for leadership development in HRD. Human Resource Development Review, 11, 156–181. doi:10.1177/153448431248211

Shuck, B. & Reio, T. G. (2011). The employee engagement landscape and HRD: How do we link theory and scholarship to current practice? *Advances in Developing Human Resources, 13,* 419–428. doi:10.1177/1523422311431153

Shuck, B., & Reio, T. (2014). Employee engagement and well-being: A moderation model and implications for practice. *Journal of Leadership & Organizational Studies, 21(1),* 43–58. doi:10.1177/1548051813494240

Shuck, B., & Rose, K. (2013). Reframing employee engagement within the context of meaning and purpose: Implications for HRD. *Advances in Developing Human Resources, 15,* 341–355. doi:10.1177/1523422313503235

Shuck, B., Twyford, D., Reio, T. W. Jr., & Shuck, A. (2014). Human resource development practices and employee engagement: Examining the connection with employee turnover intention. *Human Resource Development Quarterly, 5,* 239–270. doi:10.1002/hrdq.21190

Shuck, B., & Wollard, K. K. (2010). Employee engagement and HRD: A seminal review of the foundation. *Human Resource Development Review, 9,* 89–110. doi:10.1177/1534484309353560

Shuck, B., Zigarmi, D., & Owen, J. (2015). Psychological needs, engagement, and work intentions. *European Journal of Training and Development, 39,* 2–21. doi:10.1108/EJTD-08-2014-0061

Townsend, K., Wilkinson, A., & Burgess, J. (2014). Routes to partial success: Collaborative employment relations and employee engagement. *International Journal of Human Resource Management, 25,* 915–930. doi:10.1080/09585192.2012.743478

Valentin, C. (2014). The extra mile deconstructed: A critical and discourse perspective on employee engagement and HRD. *Human Resource Development International, 17,* 1–16. doi:10.1080/13678868.2014.932091

About the Author . . .

Dr. Le-Marlié Marais resides in Johannesburg, South Africa's largest city. Dr. Marais, also known as *Dr. Lee,* served as voluntary adjunct faculty with the University of the People, a tuition-free online university dedicated to opening access to higher education for qualified individuals. Dr. Lee co-owns and manages Njovu Strategic and Operational Advisors, a firm providing a range of services to the mining industry in Sub-Saharan Africa. She is a business professional, with 18 years of experience in the mining industry, in a variety of roles including operations management, organizational development, employee and community engagement, and business administration. Additionally, she is a certified practitioner of the MBTI Step I and Step II instruments.

Dr. Lee is a member of the Golden Key International Honor Society since 2014 as well as a member of the Delta Mu Delta International Honor Society in Business since 2016.

She is an aspiring author and published works include her dissertation: *Exploring leaders' strategies for employee engagement in the South African mining industry* and her conference paper: *Stakeholder engagement in the South African gold mining industry* presented at the Mining and Communities Solutions 2016 Conference held in Vancouver, Canada.

To reach Dr. Lee Marais for information on employee engagement, or guest speaking, please visit her **website:** http://www.njovu.co.za or **e-mail:** creativeminerlee@gmail.com

About the Company...

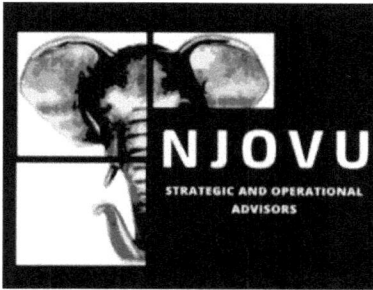

NJOVU Strategic and Operational Advisors has experienced significant industry growth since its revival in 2017. We attribute this growth to the value proposition Njovu offers clients and business partners in the African mining industry. Our organization consists of experienced professionals representing all aspects of the mining value chain, uniquely positioning Njovu to provide micro and small mining operations with all the skills traditionally fulfilled by the corporate office function at a highly competitive cost. Njovu's projects include green fields, brown fields, start-up, and turn-around projects through joint ventures, equity participation, and project management contracts. Njovu's vision is to change the face of the South African mining industry, by implementing a people-centered, learning, network-structured, hybrid-organic organizational structure suited for the knowledge era, at its operations. Our success is a result of focusing on establishing a mutually beneficial relationship between organizations and stakeholders through continuous engagement and effecting social change. Additionally, our team has the ability to apply both academic (scholar-practitioner research) and practical experience (experts in all areas of the value chain) in a labor-intensive industry when engaging with stakeholders across a broad spectrum of industries to ensure we meet and exceed stakeholder requirements for a social license to operate in our respective projects and partnerships.

For more information, please contact **email:** info@njovu.co.za or **phone: +27 84 050 4612** or **website:** https://www.njovu.co.za

CHAPTER 6

The Glocal Employee: Managing a Mosaic Workforce

Dr. Eric T. Makoni

Employee engagement is a key component to the success of an organization as engaged employees play a crucial role in achieving organizational performance especially when considering the labor costs incurred to generate organizational outcomes. Anitha (2014) posited that employee engagement is the connection between the emotional well-being of employees and their level of organizational commitment. To achieve such deep-rooted connections between employees and their organization, managers need to adopt refractive thinking and move away from traditional modes of engagement, such as using money as a motivator to engage employees, as they no longer serve the complexities of modern organizations. Huang et al. (2016) highlighted the importance of managers implementing employee engagement strategies to increase retention rates, safety climates, and job satisfaction for diverse workforces. Makoni (2019) highlighted how important it is for managers to recognize how diverse their workforce is and value engaging their employees to create high-performance workplaces that improve organizational performance.

Engaged employees are willing and happier to work towards achieving organizational goals through discretionary efforts when they are concurrently fulfilling their personal needs. Allam (2017) posited that when employees are disengaged, there is a significant level of disconnect between the organization's objectives and the performance of employees. Organizations are recognizing employees as a key resource that supports the organization's strategy to increase performance due to significant shifts in the resourcing strategies of human capital in the marketplace. Employee engagement involves organizational commitment, citizen behavior, and motivation to perform, which are all integral aspects of achieving organizational success (Albrecht, Bakker, Gruman, Macey, & Saks, 2015). Therefore, managers should develop and adopt successful employee engagement strategies to increase organizational performance using a mosaic workforce.

The Concept

The term *glocal employee* is a concept of having a workforce that has juxtaposing characteristics, reflecting the complex psychosocial and geopolitical environments of the modern industrialized knowledge-based economy. Paik, Chow, and Vance (2011) posited that through globalization managers introduced standardized practices and processes that allowed organizations to scale rapidly and increase their market share within the economy by replicating business models and practices across varying geolocations. However, when relating to managing human relationships, standardizing relationships is complex as several inherent and often conflicting factors exist that affect human relationships. The interactions between employees and management inform the relationship an employee has with the organization. Irrespective of the complex factors that influence human relationships such as culture, language and social norms, the fundamental need of employees is to have a sense of belonging and feel valued within the organization (Makoni, 2019). Therefore, the relationship between the employee and the manager becomes key in shaping how the employee engages with the organization. Managers need to adopt refractive thinking to mobilize strategies that overcome barriers to establish meaningful relationships with employees.

Birtch, Chiang, and Van Esch (2016) highlighted that the application of social exchange theory (SET) within organizational constructs emphasized the importance of organizational relationships, values, and contractual obligations to enhance organizational performance through the investment in human capital. The notion of social exchange emanated from Thibaut and Kelley's (1959) study on human behavior. Thibaut and Kelley identified mutual interdependence as the key factor that influenced social behaviors and defined social exchange as a set of outcomes based on a combination of individuals' efforts that were mutual arrangements. Homans (1961) adopted the mutual interdependence concept and coined the term *social exchange* in the context of reinforced principles, whereby the interactions between individuals occur when the activity is of mutual benefit and causes less harm or loss to the parties involved. Blau (1964) used Homans' work and applied it to an economic and utilitarian perspective where the idea was on social exchanges that resulted in anticipatory mutual benefits, where prior knowledge of the benefit was not a determining factor in participating in the exchange.

Emerson (1976) later developed SET into a framework by combining Homans and Blau's work and suggested that human relationships within organizational constructs flourished from reciprocal contingencies and rewarding processes. The processes involved the exchange of valued relationships and transactions between employees and their organizations, where reward reinforcement determined the level of transactional outcomes and commitment. According to Cropanzano, Anthony, Daniels, and Hall (2017), the foundations of SET highlight how social exchanges have either economic or socioemotional effects. Therefore, organizational managers should consider a combination of financial and psychological rewards as part of the employee engagement strategies they use to increase organizational performance.

The Challenge

Employee engagement is the relationship and level of commitment between an organization and its employees. Anitha (2014) asserted that employee engagement is a key determinant of organizational success and sustainability, notably where labor costs account for the majority of any organization's operational costs. Researchers explore employee engagement to understand the positive and negative impacts of the phenomenon on business environments, strategic goals, and organizational objectives (Alagaraja & Shuck, 2015). As a result, there is an increase in researchers' interests in exploring organizational strategies that focus on employee relationships especially in diverse workforces that encompass glocal employees. The notion of a glocal employee has brought new challenges and opportunities within organizations as employees are multigenerational, multicultural and share varying values within the workplace. The sum of those differences form a mosaic workforce where managers have to account for all types of psychosocial and personal differences in planning and decision making. Managers could adopt refractive thinking to problem-solve while accounting for inherent differences by cultivating synergies that concurrently fulfill the employee's goals and organizational objectives.

Bhuvanaiah and Raya (2014) highlighted that engaged employees enhanced job and task performance through organizational citizenship behaviors and discretionary efforts. Employee engagement, whether positive or negative, has financial implications to an organization. Organizational managers who understand the glocal employee and proactively manage a mosaic workforce create an opportunity for organizations to invest in the intellectual capital of their employees, while leveraging their diverse qualities to increase the organization's competitive advantages (Bedarkar & Pandita, 2014). Failure to understand and implement engagement strategies could lead to disengaged employees where attrition and absenteeism are rife, which negatively affects the performance and productivity of an organization (Makoni, 2019). Managers need to have a refractive thinking mindset to balance the demands of the organization's objectives with the needs of the employees and use both elements to create a cohesive environment that fosters increased performance. Therefore, organizational managers should invest in their relationship with employees and create a work environment that encourages citizenship behaviors. The result is improved productivity and performance levels for the organization.

The Determinants

Psychological Ownership

According to Bhuvanaiah and Raya (2014), intrinsic motivators form a level of psychological ownership where employees feel a sense of purpose in the organization. Psychological ownership helps in developing positive behaviors and attitudes, especially where a level of cultural difference exists, which is essential in creating an engaged workforce (Kim, & Beehr, 2017). Employees who have a heightened sense of psychological ownership exemplify increased levels of autonomy in initiating activities that advance and support organizational goals. Effectively managing a mosaic workforce leads to positive results of empowerment and comradery in the team due to increased engagement levels. Employees who experience increased feelings of psychological ownership are proactively involved in motivating and influencing other employees to achieve increased performance that supports organizational goals.

Engaged employees assume leadership roles and responsibilities and feel like they can contribute significantly to the team to influence the outcomes of the organizational goals. Han and Garg (2018) provided evidence that empowered employees exercise control over important aspects of their roles. Makoni (2019) supported empowering employees and highlighted how disempowering employees led to disengaged employees who felt as if they had no control over the outcome of their efforts. Disengaged employees felt hopeless and had no sense of ownership in their role. As a result, the engaged employees often had to pick up the slack of the underperforming employees, resulting in burnout and further disengagement. The unmotivated employees affected the team morale as well as the productivity levels of the team as a whole, resulting in further disengagement. Han and Garg emphasized that when employees feel closely linked to the organization, as in the case of psychological ownership, employees have a desire to maintain, enhance, and protect the reputation of the organization. Therefore, managers could begin to focus on instilling a sense of ownership when motivating employees by encouraging cohesion and increased goal congruence towards the organizational objectives.

Job Resources

Brenninkmeijer and Hekkert-Koning (2015) defined job resources as the physical, social, and organizational aspects of a job that function in achieving organizational goals while stimulating personal development and growth. The consensus among glocal employees is that job resources are a crucial employee engagement strategy that helps employees excel in their job role. Managers should provide sufficient resourcing for employees to function in their job roles. Makoni (2019) highlighted that building trust makes employees feel more engaged especially within a safe and supportive space were glocal employees are creative and innovative while expressing their views at work. Slemp, Kern, and Vella-Brodrick (2015) posited that managers who provide feedback, job control, and support could improve work engagement. Employees become more motivated and willing to approach management when they encounter workplace issues. As a result, employees feel comfortable with sharing their grievances and provide solutions in overcoming organizational challenges. Managers could focus on understanding the needs of their employees to ensure they provide the appropriate job resourcing that could potentially increase productivity, thereby improving organizational performance. However, under resourcing remains a pertinent issue that stifles supportive, nurtured, and well-resourced environments. Managers could focus on facilitating job resources as a strategy that plays an intrinsic motivational role in initiating the organization's willingness to invest in their employees so that they can reach their full potential.

Leadership

Managers who aim to improve organizational performance need to have a culture of continuous improvement and development as trends, technologies, and stakeholder preferences continuously evolve over time (Elsbach & Stigliani, 2018). Leadership is a vital catalyst that could make an organization successful. According to Karunathilake (2016), leadership is the art or process of influencing and inspiring people to perform assigned tasks willingly, efficiently, and competently. Receiving ideas from the workforce about what employees would prefer to do, then aligning those ideas with the organizational needs helps to keep glocal employees motivated and engaged. Managers need to practice an equitable decision-making process to ensure that there is fairness and clarity among employees. Listening to what improvements employees would like to make could also improve engagement and provide transparency on how the organization aims to support its employees in exchange for their discretionary efforts. Management responses to issues raised also need to be transparent, and consultation with senior leadership needs to involve the team members that raised the issues.

Salas, Shuffler, Thayer, Bedwell, and Lazzara (2015) highlighted the importance of leadership in harnessing employee efforts through teamwork to fulfill organizational goals. Managers with leadership skills could improve performance efficiencies within an organization, which positively influences the achievement of organizational goals. Sahu, Pathardikar, and Kumar (2018) emphasized how managers who exercise leadership skills in their role could foster a culture of cooperation whereby employees have a positive attitude towards fulfilling organizational goals. Organizations that have a strategic direction assist in establishing a systematic intervention approach that managers could use to improve the organization's outcomes. Mittal and Dhar (2015) also posited that managers need to showcase leadership behaviors that build an environment in which every employee develops and excels. Managers experience conflicting priorities between shareholder return and employee satisfaction, especially in organizations where there is a lack of flexibility in providing autonomy to management. Makoni (2019) identified that the majority of successful engagement initiatives have to be manager-led to keep employees motivated and engaged. Through organizational leadership, managers have the potential to influence and drive group efforts towards accomplishing organizational goals. Therefore, managers need to exercise leadership to execute successful engagement strategies that improve organizational performance.

Training and Development

Bell, Tannenbaum, Ford, Noe, and Kraiger (2017) described professional training as programs and strategies that help employees learn specific knowledge or skills that improve performance in their roles. Professional development is more expansive and focuses on the employees' professional growth and future performance, while supporting the current demands of the role. Hanaysha and Tahir (2016) prescribed training and development programs to help the organization to retain the right talent, as engaged employees have a direct effect on the bottom line. Hiring top talented employees takes time and money; how managers engage and develop that talent from the time employees join the organization impacts retention and organizational growth. Mason (2018) posited that high-impact training and development programs were a result of careful planning and alignment processes. Makoni (2019) further highlighted the importance of listening to employees' goals so that their tasks align with their goals, furthering goal congruence with organizational objectives. Managers will need to develop inclusive training programs that accommodate the diverse workforce while remaining relevant to the organization's objectives.

Hanaysha and Tahir posited that measurable learning objectives are the foundation for evaluating an initiative's impact. Introducing a champions program whereby employees act as role models and experts in different aspects of the organization is an initiative that provides a measurable outcome, as the objective is to upskill the individual in the area requiring development. Furthermore, employees who have a sense of ownership in their job roles have responsibility towards certain aspects of their role that affects the organizations performance. Employee training and development programs are key differentiators of successful organizations as the battle for top talent becomes more competitive. Prioritizing employee development results in higher retention rates as glocal employees feel supported in their professional development. Managers need to prioritize training and development opportunities to equip mosaic workforces with the right skills and expertise to excel in their job roles. Managers need to think outside of the box and design inclusive programs that empower the workforce to excel in their roles, so they feel a sense of fulfilment in their roles.

Rewards and Recognition

Appreciation is a fundamental human need. Employee recognition is the timely, informal, or formal acknowledgment of a person or team's behavior that is beyond reasonable expectations, which supports the organization's goals and values (Chiniara & Bentein, 2016). The consensus among glocal employees is that rewards and recognition is a key employee engagement strategy that increases organizational performance. Lu, Lu, Gursoy, and Neale (2016) posited that employees respond to appreciation expressed through recognition of their work as recognition confirms that others value their work. Glocal employees within mosaic workforces want respect and want their contributions to be valued and recognized. Managers who provide regular praise and recognition to team members for their efforts see improved performance results within the team. Valued employees have higher satisfaction and productivity levels as they feel motivated to maintain or improve their work (Potoski & Callery, 2018). Praise and recognition are essential to achieve an outstanding and high performing workplace. Ghosh et al. (2016) posited that employees feel the need for recognition as an individual or member of a group and want to feel a sense of achievement for work well done.

The lack of support from senior management in promoting reward and recognition programs is often a barrier to engagement. Managers lack the backing of senior management influence to effectively roll out engagement initiatives and embed successful engagement practices to be part of the organization's policies (Makoni, 2019). Managers will need to exercise refractive thinking to use existing resources such as weekly newsletter shout-outs for recognizing employees for their efforts during the week or engaging the employees to collectively determine the rewards that are meaningful and worthy of attainment. Bear, Slaughter, Mantz, and Farley-Ripple (2017) described intrinsic rewards as the feel-good emotions people get from excelling in their role, enjoying tasks, feelings about the opportunities available to them, and pride in doing a good job. It is important to address disengaged employees strategically to avoid tarnishing the team morale. Patterson and Zibarras (2017) encouraged managers to treat problems as opportunities for innovation, and to encourage people to try new approaches that may improve productivity. If employees are unhappy and are not given encouragement, listened to or noticed, then they do not want to be at work and are not going to perform. Therefore, it is essential for managers to create a positive workplace culture in which employees are rewarded and recognized for their efforts to improve employee engagement, thereby improving organizational performance.

The Opportunity

Organizational managers have an influential role in creating an engaging work environment. Anitha (2014) highlighted that once organizational managers understand the key ingredients in creating an engaged mosaic workforce and how work environments are influential in improving levels of engagement, employees can then feel safe, take supported risks, and be willing to innovate to create a high-performing workplace. While many factors contribute to employee engagement, Eldor and Vigoda-Gadot (2017) identified work centrality, feedback, recognition, and empowerment as key factors that influence employees to have a sense of belonging while feeling valued, all of which have a direct impact and influence on organizational performance. Implementing employee engagement strategies could positively contribute to social change through the development and investment of glocal employees. Albrecht, Bakker, Gruman, Macey, and Saks (2015) posited that employees are critical assets of any organizations as their significant intrinsic value has both economic and competitive advantages for any organization. Employee engagement is one such strategy that ensures investment in human capital, and that investment translates into improved organizational performance.

Makoni (2019) highlighted how managers need to be proactive in developing engagement initiatives that are relevant and tailored to their teams. Understanding the team culture has a significant influence when designing the appropriate initiatives that could keep the team motivated. Managers need to adopt significant human resource management strategies aimed at recruiting and retaining skilled professionals. Pivoting is a key refractive thinking strategy that helps manage a mosaic workforce as managers could apply principles and processes that are relevant to the employees, as opposed to prescribing to archaic, rigid practices riddled with legacy issues. Previously, the performance and profitability of the organization determined the engagement strategies for the organization. In current times, a collaborative approach is necessary to engage individuals from diverse ethnic and cultural backgrounds as well as individuals who have diverse abilities and preferences in relation to their flexibility within the workplace. Managers need to understand that what may have worked with one group of employees historically may not always be applicable with a different cohort in the present. The key is to recruit employees who have goal congruence and match the job fit so that they can grow and nurture a mosaic workforce that understands and drives organizational goals and performance while fulfilling their own goals. Onboarding programs need to be robust enough to equip employees with the right skills to perform within their roles. Managers who foster job skilling empower employees in their roles and provide them with a sense of psychological ownership. Job matching also fosters goal congruence between the employee's goals and the organization's goals, which increases productivity and performance levels.

Conclusion

The purpose of the chapter was to explore employee engagement strategies that some managers use to increase organizational performance in a mosaic workforce. SET provided a conceptual framework to explore the five determinants of employee engagement which were psychological ownership, job resources, leadership, training and development, and rewards and recognition. Makoni (2019) highlighted the importance of mutually beneficial relationships among managers and glocal employees. Managers have an opportunity to establish engagement strategies that enhance and influence mosaic workforces to provide discretionary efforts in their roles. The workforce landscape is continuously evolving, but the fundamental need for any employee is to feel connected and have a sense of belonging in the workplace. When employees feel involved, heard, and motivated in their job roles they increase their productivity and provide quality outcomes that could improve organizational performance. Effective managers could employ refractive thinking to create a safe climate for employees to fulfill their needs while improving operational efficiencies and organizational performance.

THOUGHTS FROM THE ACADEMIC ENTREPRENEUR

The problem to be solved:

- Disengaged employees have a negative impact on organizational performance.

- Some managers lack employee engagement strategies to engage and manage a mosaic workforce so as to increase organizational performance.

The goals:

- Understanding how to engage a diverse workforce

- To explore employee engagement strategies that some managers use to increase organizational performance.

The questions to ask:

- What employee engagement strategies do some managers use to increase organizational performance?

Today's Business Application:

- Managers need to recognize the value of human capital as an essential organizational strategy that drives organizational performance.

- Managers need to adopt significant human resource management strategies aimed at recruiting and retaining skilled professionals in the organization.

- Effective managers are proactive in developing engagement initiatives that are relevant and tailored to their team.

- Engagement initiatives are better led from a bottom-up approach as opposed to a top-down approach to be effective and to have an immediate impact.

- Managers need to understand employees' goals to match them to the right job as well as provide relevant training and development programs and support.

- Managers need to continuously review their human resource strategies to ensure that the current human resource practices are relevant to the current workforce and the organization's needs.

REFERENCES

Alagaraja, M., & Shuck, B. (2015). Exploring organizational alignment-employee engagement linkages and impact on individual performance: A conceptual model. *Human Resource Development Review, 14,* 17–37. doi:10.1177/1534484314549455

Albrecht, S. L., Bakker, A. B., Gruman, J. A., Macey, W. H., & Saks, A. M. (2015). Employee engagement, human resource management practices and competitive advantage: An integrated approach. *Journal of Organizational Effectiveness: People and Performance, 2,* 7–35. doi:10.1108/JOEPP-08-2014-0042

Allam, Z. (2017). Employee disengagement: A fatal consequence to organization and its ameliorative measures. *International Review of Management and Marketing, 7*(2), 49–52. Retrieved from http://www.econjournals.com

Anitha, J. (2014). Determinants of employee engagement and their impact on employee performance. *International Journal of Productivity and Performance Management, 63,* 308–323. doi:10.1108/IJPPM-01-2013-0008

Bailey, C., Madden, A., Alfes, K., Fletcher, L., Robinson, D., Holmes, J., . . . & Currie, G. (2015). Evaluating the evidence on employee engagement and its potential benefits to NHS staff: A narrative synthesis of the literature. *Health Services and Delivery Research, 3,* 14–24. doi:10.3310/hsdr03260

Bear, G. G., Slaughter, J. C., Mantz, L. S., & Farley-Ripple, E. (2017). Rewards, praise, and punitive consequences: Relations with intrinsic and extrinsic motivation. *Teaching and Teacher Education, 65*(1), 10–20. doi:10.1016/j.tate.2017.03.001

Bedarkar, M., & Pandita, D. (2014). A study on the drivers of employee engagement impacting employee performance. *Procedia-Social and Behavioral Sciences, 133,* 106–115. doi:10.1016/j.sbspro.2014.04.174

Bell, B. S., Tannenbaum, S. I., Ford, J. K., Noe, R. A., & Kraiger, K. (2017). 100 years of training and development research: What we know and where we should go. *Journal of Applied Psychology, 102,* 305–323. doi:10.1037/apl0000142

Bhuvanaiah, T., & Raya, R. P. (2014). Employee engagement: Key to organizational success. *SCMS Journal of Indian Management, 11,* 61–71. Retrieved from https://www.scms.edu.in/journal

Bin, A. S. (2016). The relationship between job satisfaction, job performance and employee engagement: An explorative study. *Issues in Business Management and Economics, 4,* 1–8. doi:10.15739/IBME.16.001

Birtch, T. A., Chiang, F. F., & Van Esch, E. (2016). A social exchange theory framework for understanding the job characteristics–job outcomes relationship: The mediating role of psychological contract fulfillment. *International Journal of*

Human Resource Management, 27, 1217–1236. doi:10.1080/09585192.2015.10
69752

Blau, P. M. (1964). *Exchange and power in social life.* New Brunswick, NJ: Wiley.

Brenninkmeijer, V., & Hekkert-Koning, M. (2015). To craft or not to craft: The relationships between regulatory focus, job crafting and work outcomes. *Career Development International, 20,* 147–162. doi:10.1108/CDI-12-2014-0162

Chiniara, M., & Bentein, K. (2016). Linking servant leadership to individual performance: Differentiating the mediating role of autonomy, competence and relatedness need satisfaction. *Leadership Quarterly, 27,* 124–141. doi:10.1016/j. leaqua.2015.08.004

Cropanzano, R., Anthony, E. L., Daniels, S. R., & Hall, A. V. (2017). Social exchange theory: A critical review with theoretical remedies. *Academy of Management Annals, 11,* 479–516. doi:10.5465/annals.2015.0099

Eldor, L., & Vigoda-Gadot, E. (2017). The nature of employee engagement: Rethinking the employee–organization relationship. *International Journal of Human Resource Management, 28,* 526–552. doi:10.1080/09585192.2016.118 0312

Elsbach, K. D., & Stigliani, I. (2018). Design thinking and organizational culture: A review and framework for future research. *Journal of Management, 44,* 2274–2306. doi:10.1177/0149206317744252

Emerson, R. M. (1976). Social exchange theory. *Annual Review of Sociology, 2,* 335–362. doi:10.1146/annurev.so.02.080176.002003

Han, K. S., & Garg, P. (2018). Workplace democracy and psychological capital: A paradigm shift in workplace. *Management Research Review, 41,* 1088–1116. doi:10.1108/MRR-11-2016-0267

Hanaysha, J., & Tahir, P. R. (2016). Examining the effects of employee empowerment, teamwork, and employee training on job satisfaction. *Procedia-Social and Behavioral Sciences, 219,* 272–282. doi:10.1016/j.sbspro.2016.05.016

Homans, C. G. (1961). *Social behavior; Its elementary forms.* New York City, NY: Harcourt, Brace, & World.

Huang, Y. H., Lee, J., McFadden, A. C., Murphy, L. A., Robertson, M. M., Cheung, J. H., & Zohar, D. (2016). Beyond safety outcomes: An investigation of the impact of safety climate on job satisfaction, employee engagement and turnover using social exchange theory as the theoretical framework. *Applied Ergonomics, 55,* 248–257. doi:10.1016/j.apergo.2015.10.007

Karunathilake, L. P. V. (2016). The impact of leaders' characteristics and their behavior to the employee performance in the hotel industry in Sri Lanka. *Wayamba Journal of Management, 4,* 9–19. doi:10.4038/wjm.v4i2.7457

Kim, M., & Beehr, T. A. (2017). Self-efficacy and psychological ownership mediate the effects of empowering leadership on both good and bad employee behaviors. *Journal of Leadership & Organizational Studies, 24,* 466–478. doi:10.1177/1548051817702078

Lu, L., Lu, A. C. C., Gursoy, D., & Neale, N. R. (2016). Work engagement, job satisfaction, and turnover intentions: A comparison between supervisors and line-level employees. *International Journal of Contemporary Hospitality Management, 28,* 737–761. doi:10.1108/IJCHM-07–2014–0360

Mason, P. (2018). Clackamas county public health: Employee engagement in quality improvement and performance management activities. *Journal of Public Health Management and Practice, 24,* S22-S24. doi:10.1097/PHH.0000000000000705

Mittal, S., & Dhar, R. L. (2015). Transformational leadership and employee creativity: mediating role of creative self-efficacy and moderating role of knowledge sharing. *Management Decision, 53,* 894–910. doi:10.1108/MD-07–2014–0464

Paik, Y., Chow, I. H. S., & Vance, C. M. (2011). Interaction effects of globalization and institutional forces on international HRM practice: Illuminating the convergence?divergence debate. *Thunderbird International Business Review, 53,* 647–659. doi:10.1002/tie.20440

Patterson, F., & Zibarras, L. D. (2017). Selecting for creativity and innovation potential: implications for practice in healthcare education. *Advances in Health Sciences Education, 22,* 417–428. doi:10.1007/s10459–016–9731–4

Potoski, M., & Callery, P. J. (2018). Peer communication improves environmental employee engagement programs: Evidence from a quasi-experimental field study. *Journal of Cleaner Production, 172,* 1486–1500. doi:10.1016/j.jclepro.2017.10.252

Sahu, S., Pathardikar, A., & Kumar, A. (2018). Transformational leadership and turnover. *Leadership & Organization Development Journal, 39,* 82–99. doi:10.1108/lodj-12–2014–0243

Salas, E., Shuffler, M. L., Thayer, A. L., Bedwell, W. L., & Lazzara, E. H. (2015). Understanding and improving teamwork in organizations: A scientifically based practical guide. *Human Resource Management, 54,* 599–622. doi:10.1002/hrm.21628

Slemp, G. R., Kern, M. L., & Vella-Brodrick, D. A. (2015). Workplace well-being: The role of job crafting and autonomy support. *Psychology of Well-being, 5*(1), 1–17. doi:10.1186/s13612–015–0034-y

Thibaut, J. W., & Kelley, H. H. (1959). *The social psychology of groups.* Oxford, England: Wiley.

About the Author . . .

Dr. Eric T Makoni resides in Melbourne, Australia. Dr. Eric has several accredited degrees; a Bachelor of Science in Nursing from Murdoch University, a Master of Public Health from Charles Darwin University; a Master of Business Administration (MBA) from the University of Newcastle and a Doctor of Business Administration (DBA) in Healthcare Management from Walden University. Dr. Eric has 12 years professional experience in healthcare with various clinical / administrative and managerial roles held in hospitals across Australia and Saudi Arabia specializing in Acute Medical, Surgical, Pediatrics, Ambulatory Care, and Emergency Departments.

Dr. Eric aims to be an influential leader who can inform sustainable and valuable change through the understanding of health systems, business strategies, and models of care. He continuously drives change and excellence within healthcare and is passionate about advancing the quadruple approach in business practices to optimize processes and improve service outcomes through human capital and glocal employees as human capital.

Dr. Eric is an active member of the Golden Key International Honor Society and Delta Mu Delta International Business Honor Society. Dr. Eric has also been recognized for academic excellence by receiving the NT African Australian Academic Excellence Award and volunteers as a humanitarian for not for profit charity organizations.

To reach Dr. Eric T Makoni for additional information please visit his **Linked In profile** https://www.linkedin.com/in/dr-eric-makoni-130b0b114 or **e-mail:** makoni.eric@gmail.com

CHAPTER 7

Global Leadership and Cross-Cultural Competencies: Leading Beyond Awareness

Dr. Gail Ade & Dr. Tokunbo Majaro

As the globalized, knowledge-driven and technologically progressive economy advances extensive opportunities for free-trade, investments, partnerships, and cheaper labor, organizations continue to seek new opportunities for financial growth, operational efficiency, and innovative advantages across the globe (Flynn, 2019). In the 21st-century boundaryless society, organizations operate in culturally distinct conditions and hiring multicultural employees to gain competitive advantage. Thus, resulting in a notable demographic shift in modern workforce composition. Conventionally, apparent differences in age, race, gender, identity, religion, social status, and ethnicity, characterized workforce diversity (Mor-Barak, 2017). However, the modern workforce is more diverse than ever; spanning across different regions, generations, cultures, orientation, and dynamics. With an open pathway to previously inaccessible trade markets and socioeconomic transformations, the employees of global and multinational companies (MNCs) are socially, culturally, and geographically dispersed with different values, beliefs, mindset, and customs (Fitzsimmons, Liao, & Thomas, 2017; Sebastian Reiche, Bird, Mendenhall, & Osland, 2017). Hence, the effective management of such multicultural heterogeneity underpins the need for agile leadership proficiencies and dexterous cross-cultural competencies (Jordan, Ferris, & Lamont, 2019).

As MNCs experience heightened levels of globalized inter-connectedness and interdependence, the nuances of human interactions and variances in values (social and cultural), make situational ambiguities and humanistic complexities the modern-day reality (Fitzsimmons, Liao, & Thomas, 2017; Landesz, 2018). According to Lane, Maznevski, and Mendenhall (2004), operating in foreign markets and competing globally embodies (a) added complexity because of multiplicity across different dimensions; (b) interdependence between multiple and global stakeholders; (c) ambiguities in practices, relationships and values; and (d) flux (instability) because of cross-cultural integration. Irrespective of domain or size, these dynamic complexities do impact not only global strategic and operational efficiency but also presents unique challenges for cross-cultural management. Thus, the need for globally competent and culturally intelligent leaders is inherently crucial. As a result, organizations continuously seek leaders who can successfully transcend cross-cultural barriers and effectively manage the combined interplay of worldwide stakeholders, e.g., employees, customers, suppliers, and competitors (Lima Neves & Amélia Tomei, 2017; Sebastian Reiche et al., 2017).

The multifaceted value of international commerce makes global leadership paradigm indispensable to researchers and organizational development (OD) practitioners seeking to determine the key competencies that leaders need to thrive globally and effectively manage the 21st century diverse workforce (Flynn, 2019). Global leadership is the ability to influence others "to adopt a shared vision through structures and methods that facilitate positive change while fostering individual and collective growth in a context characterized by significant levels of complexity, flow, and presence" (Mendenhall et al., 2013, p. 500).

In the context of this chapter, global leadership involves taking indigenous capabilities beyond national and cultural boundaries, i.e., engaging globally and culturally diverse stakeholders for sustainable outcomes. Lima Neves and Amélia Tomei (2017) characterized global leaders beyond senior-level executives to include business leaders who employ diverse workforce, and are involved with stakeholders inclusivity, multicultural collaborations, and cross-cultural engagement. These classifications also include expatriates, i.e., leaders who leave their home country to work in the host country.

What Competencies are Required for Global Leaders to Succeed in Geographically and Culturally Diverse Business Environments?

A plethora of research indicated that the embodied proficiencies of skilled global leaders include: global orientation; sensitivity to complex conditions; openness to new experiences; flexibility in behaviors; productive intercommunication; embracing cultural diversity; cultivating multicultural relationships; integration and adaptability; tolerance during ambiguity; continuous learning (Daher, 2015; Gunkel, Schlaegel, & Taras, 2016; Young, Haffejee, & Corsun, 2018). These competencies are comprehensively universal to match the intricacies of interpersonal dealings in geographically and culturally diverse business environments. However, the focus of this chapter of the refractive thinker includes cultural intelligence, global mindset, emotional intelligence, awareness, mindfulness, and authentic leadership competencies.

Cultural Intelligence

As a phenomenon deeply embedded in social and psychological construct, understanding culture, cultural differences, and cross-cultural dynamics are operative competencies for global leaders. According to Hofstede (1980), culture is the normative beliefs, lifestyle, assumptions, shared values, morals and outlook that distinguishes a particular group, nation, or society from others (as cited in Gunkel et al., 2016). The ability to espouse cognitive flexibility, inductive analogical reasoning, as well as the flexibility to acclimatize with different cultures, is the unique strategic value of cross-cultural intelligence (Jyoti & Kour, 2017). *Cultural Intelligence* (CQ) is the "capability of an individual to effectively function in situations characterized by cultural diversity" (Ang & Van Dyne, 2015, p. 3). Cultural intelligence encompasses skills that empower leaders to transfer social skills from one cultural context to another to mitigate conflicts and apply appropriate leadership behaviors as situationally needed (Anderson & Bergdolt, 2017). According to Jyoti and Kour (2017), leaders with higher CQ are better equipped to deal with confusing situations because of their ability to think deeply and make appropriate cultural adjustments. The CQ framework is multifaceted, consisting of metacognitive, cognitive, motivational, and behavioral components (Chao, Takeuchi, & Farh, 2017).

Metacognitive CQ refers to the acquisition of cultural knowledge and influence on the reasoning aptitudes (Chao et al., 2017; Young et al., 2018). Individuals with high levels of metacognitive CQ have a deep sense of cultural perception and can adjust when interacting with people from other cultures accordingly (Varela, 2018). *Cognitive CQ* is the knowledge about practices, norms, and beliefs of several cultures often acquired through training, education, and personal experiences (Chao et al., 2017). Individuals with high levels of cognitive CQ maintain preemptive tactics, which are vital for understanding the distinctions between diverse cultures (Ang & Van Dyne, 2015; Ott & Michailova, 2018). *Motivational CQ* relates to how genuinely determined a person is to understand various cultures and effectively adapt, i.e., the intrinsic desire to learn about other cultures (Chao et al., 2017; Young et al., 2018). *Behavioral CQ* is the comprehension of physical dynamics that are relevant to different cultures and the ability to exhibit respectful verbal and nonverbal behaviors during intercultural encounters (Chao et al., 2017). Leaders with higher motivational and behavioral CQ are enthused to participate in cross-cultural interactions, such as communicating, networking, bridging divides, and sharing knowledge in a diverse cultural environment (Ang & Van Dyne, 2015; Young et al., 2018).

Several researchers underpin the business impact of CQ competencies in leveraging cultural diversity for global economic and innovative solutions; CQ has been associated with better decision-making abilities, quality work, idea sharing, collaboration, and performance optimization (Turner et al., 2019). CQ positively affects the outcome of work performance and human behaviors (Chao et al., 2017); competitive advantage, increased profits, and successful global expansions directly correlate with a high level of cultural intelligence (Livemore & Soon, 2015). Openness to dissimilarity, cognitive flexibility (broad problem-solving perspectives), and self-efficacy are other vital attributes of culturally intelligent leaders (Ang & Van Dyne, 2015; Chao et al., 2017). These different components of CQ vastly underscore that CQ relates to a myriad of cultural situations, thereby increasing the capacity of global leaders to engage employees from diverse cultural backgrounds effectively.

Global Mindset

A commonly cited attribute of global leadership is global mindset or global orientation, which is the underlying competency that leaders need to conceptualize global strategies and successfully contextualize its integration locally (Lima Neves & Amélia

Tomei, 2017). Levy, Taylor, Boyacugiller, and Beechler (2007) defined global mindset as "a highly complex cognitive construct characterized by an openness to and articulation of multiple cultural and strategic realities on both global and local levels, and the cognitive ability to mediate and integrate across this multiplicity" (p. 27). Essentially, a global mindset is the cognitive capability to understand the nuances of varying perspectives (*differentiation*), consolidate the different viewpoints (*integration*), and utilize the derived knowledge effectively (Chandwani et al., 2016; Levy et al., 2007). According to Jiang, Ananthram, and Li (2018), leaders with mindset possess three overarching capabilities to (a) process and analyze global business information; (b) use globally relevant information during decision-making; and (c) foster relationships with global and culturally-diverse stakeholders.

A global mindset is like a cognitive filter that intrinsically incites *cosmopolitanism* (appreciation of different cultures) and *cognitive complexity* (distinguishing varying situations and integrating different constructs successfully) (Jiang, Ananthram, & Li, 2018; Levy et al., 2007). Therefore, leaders with global mindsets have a ubiquitous outlook and inclusive orientation, which are the novel hallmarks of successful global leaders (Levy et al., 2007). Also, having a global mindset transmutes ethnocentric thinking, and sensitizes leaders to multicultural diversity, enhance creativity, and boost innovation (Jaradat & Iurian, 2019). For multinational companies, a global mindset combines cultural intelligence and global business orientation, consequently, an indispensable baseline that transcends the boundaries and barriers of global expansion (Chandwani, Agrawal, & Kedia, 2016; Lima Neves & Amélia Tomei, 2017). As a result, a global mindset is not only quintessential for internationalization into the 21st-century heterogeneous marketplace, but a strategic pathway for organizations and global leaders to thrive beyond survival (Chandwani et al., 2016; Levy et al., 2007).

Emotional Intelligence

Emotional intelligence (EI), a fundamental precept to effective leadership, is the ability to understand and regulate emotions (personal and others), as well as, the capacity to utilize emotions to positively influence desired performance or outcome (Darvishmotevali, Altinay, & De Vita, 2018; Goleman, Boyatzis, & McKee, 2013). Researchers often associate CQ and Emotional intelligence (EI) because of the interconnected proficiencies that distinguish outstanding leaders from average leaders. Emotional intelligence requires the ability to sense emotions correctly, facilitate logic by emotions, effectively discern the trigger of emotions, and regulate emotions at appropriate frequency during interactions or encounters (Darvishmotevali et al., 2018). Emotional intelligence consists of two major categories; personal competency (self-awareness and self-regulation) and social competency (social awareness, social influence, and relationship management skills) (Goleman, 1998, as cited in Mathews, 2016, p. 45). Pragmatically, a self-aware leader has a thorough understanding of personal strengths and limitations (Adewoye, 2013). Understanding nonverbal communication or hints, especially from individuals from other cultures, as well as actively seeking out information on varied cultures, requires emotional awareness and self?management (Darvishmotevali et al., 2018). An emotionally intelligent leader can self-regulate (control feelings and impulses) and socially demonstrate compassion, empathy, and consideration (Forsyth, 2015). These components of emotional intelligence are all fundamental to leadership success in a global environment.

Awareness and Mindfulness

Awareness, the foundational principle of global leadership, global mindset, CQ, EQ, and multicultural competencies, appear to be the basic tenets for succeeding across geographic, socio-cultural, and economic diversity (Ott & Michailova, 2018). The multidimensions of the competency constructs mentioned above all share overlapping characteristics, which is personal introspection (awareness). *Awareness* is the capacity to examine personal values and beliefs about differences to become more accommodating and less apprehensive of others (Lippincott, 2018). Iheduru-Anderson (2015) asserted that awareness occurs when leaders are conscious of personal feelings and preemptive reactions. Tuleja (2014) showed that beyond self-awareness is the cognizance of immediate circumstances and the ability to adjust appropriately (Mindfulness). *Mindfulness* is the metacognitive capability to use reflection as a connection between knowledge and behavior, without judgment or prejudice (Tuleja, 2014). For global leaders, mindfulness betokens presence, open-mind-edness, active participation (rather than just passively receiving information), and intentional engagement of culturally diverse stakeholders (Chandwani et al., 2016). In addition to the ability to accept contradictions and negative feedback, mindfulness alleviates abrupt reactions, aggressive behaviors, and stereotypical prejudice (Heppner & Kernis, 207; Tuleja, 2014). In intercultural encounters, mindfulness can reduce cross?cultural misunder-standings, enhance interpersonal relationships, improve social behavior, and increase the capacity to manage interpersonal conflicts (Chandwani et al., 2016). Thus, mindfulness through awareness empowers global leaders to cultivate effective social relationships with diverse cultures.

How Can 21st-Century Leaders Culturally and Socially Adapt Without Losing Authenticity?

MNCs are susceptible to the demands of globally diverse stakeholders and the realities of globalization, i.e., endless change and rapid adaptation to constantly evolving changes (Mathews, 2016). Without authenticity, leaders can yield to the disruptive pressures and become adrift, despite numerous global laws. Before-mentioned dilemmas are the reason why integrity, ethical awareness, and genuineness are pivotal to the strategic ability of authentic leaders to maintain moral standards, build employee loyalty, and establish trust. Several studies associate trust with successful business outcomes, such as job satisfaction, optimal performance, and creativity (Giallonardo, Wong, & Iwasiw, 2010; Majaro, 2018). Hence, culturally competent leaders need to be authentic and morally grounded, irrespective of geographical location and cultural environment.

Through authentic leadership theory, global leaders can maintain authenticity and stay morally grounded via ethical reasoning, transparency, consistency, and moral integrity (Landesz, 2018). Authenticity for global leaders espouses self-awareness (mindful personal introspection); balanced processing (objective evaluation of information before taking actions); internalized moral perspective (self-regulated integrity shaped by values and ethical standards, not organizational and societal factors); and relational transparency (genuine interactions and willingness to share information) (Landesz, 2018; Villarreal, 2014). Authentic leaders should appropriate psychological meaningfulness to gain legitimate influence, build stable relationships, organizational commitment, and improve employee engagement (Sidani & Rowe, 2018). With authenticity, multicultural leaders can foster global sustainable success.

Workplace Strategies for Increasing Global Leadership and Cultural Competency

Global leadership and multicultural competencies (a combination of intercultural and cross-cultural competency construct) are continuously expanding to address the increasing needs of the ever-evolving global business environment. As a result, there are no conceivable undertakings that can help global leaders or multinational organizations master all the cultures in the world (Turner et al., 2019). Through refractive thinking, nonetheless, organizations can combine the ensuing professional development programs, as well as multicultural and cultural intelligence training in various social contexts.

Inclusive and engaging culture. Given the inherent complexities of the 21st-century business environment, corporations have to be intentional towards global diversity and cultural inclusivity to cultivate an organizational climate of acceptance, open-mindedness, cohesiveness and intercultural appreciation (Glasener, Martell, & Posselt, 2018; Meng, Reber, & Rogers, 2017). Contemporary companies should leverage cultural diversity for a competitive market edge by sustaining a culturally inclusive and engaging environment that guarantees equal treatment and opportunities for all employees (Ade, Majaro, & Poshi, 2019). To elevate such a premise, it is imperative that MNCs become mindful of how intra-and-inter workplace culture, internal practices, policies, and norms, impact diverse employees throughout the organization (Darvishmotevali et al., 2018; Glasener et al., 2018). To encourage employee engagement, collaborations, social interactions, teamwork, and working alliances, organizations should maximize the role of Employee Resource Groups (known as ERGs, employee resource networks, or affinity groups). ERGs are voluntary employee-led inclusive groups or engagement platforms that offer safe space/community "to discuss issues, voice concerns, increase visibility, and receive learning and development support" (Dutton, 2018, p. 20). Most importantly, engaging and nurturing an inclusive work culture also needs ongoing effort and constant reflection to instill the appreciation and respect for cultural diversity throughout the organization (Bartel-Radic & Giannelloni, 2017; Iheduru-Anderson, 2015).

Training and professional development. Because there is no one-size-fits-all approach to gain professional development, multicultural competencies development requires broad-based strategies that are humanist, multidisciplinary, and transdisciplinary (Chai et al., 2016). Experts often use a myriad of diagnostic instruments, surveys, assessment tools and customizable developmental programs to assess competency and proficiency baseline; identify strengths and weaknesses, improvement training for areas of deficiencies, and periodic reassessment to sustain results (Daher, 2015; Walker, 2018). For global leadership competency development, several researchers recommended the combined use of competency inventories, surveys, and assessments targeting cognitive, social, experiential, and learning models to develop flexible, adaptable, socially responsible global and culturally competent leaders (Azevedo & Shane, 2019; Mendenhall et al., 2013; Walker, 2018). Some other best practices include the diversity training using cultural simulations, didactic-experiential approach, with culture?specific and cross-cultural programs that target metacognitive, motivational and behavioral paradigm (Bernardo & Presbitero, 2018; Daher, 2015; Walker, 2018). Di Stefano, Cataldo, and Laghetti (2019) suggested ongoing diversity education and cultural competence training using case studies, group discussions, and role-playing exercises to simulate communication and multicultural team-building skills.

Real-world experience. Beyond training and workshops, companies should integrate cultural diversity practices with global strength-based mobility initiatives like short-term assignments in foreign business units, interdepartmental rotations, study abroad opportunities, international training events/conferences, or cross-functional team projects (Alon et al., 2018; Iheduru-Anderson,

2015; Tuleja, 2014). Alon et al. (2018) posited that international mobility experiences would familiarize employees and emerging leaders with diverse cultures and create an opportunity to learn foreign languages and better communication skills. Cross-cultural hands-on experiences will also cultivate a global mindset by helping leaders become more reflective and culturally sensitive (Tuleja, 2014). Global exposure to cross-cultural environments will enable learning, networking, and sharing information, which will, in turn, improve empathy, flexibility, mindfulness, and appreciation of others who are different (Iheduru-Anderson, 2015).

Mentoring and coaching. A great way to promote intercultural training, relationship building and social-cultural capital within the organizations is to foster knowledge-transfer and succession planning through mentoring (Alon et al., 2018). Culturally competent leaders can mentor emerging leaders and provide expatriates with culture-specific training to improve leadership experiences in host countries (Vaccaro & Camba, 2018). Mentoring will also offer real-world opportunities to integrate and adapt to foreign cultures from observing and interacting with culturally competent leaders (Vaccaro & Camba, 2018). Aside from real-world and mentoring experience, it also crucial for global leaders to recognize the impact of prejudice, blind spots, stereotypes and bias on behaviors, decision-making processes, and choices (D'Almeida & Grossi, 2016; Dalton & Villagran, 2018). Leadership coaching can be a great training tool for enhancing self-reflexivity (awareness of explicit and implicit predispositions) of global and multicultural leaders. Incorporating coaching programs can also help global or domestic leaders uncover and manage unconscious biases, blind spots, and prejudice (Johnson & Jackson Williams, 2015; Dalton & Villagran, 2018: Vaccaro & Camba, 2018).

Continuous learning philosophy. Developing and maintaining a culturally competent leadership pipeline compels organizations to make talent development a part of the recruitment, advancement, and retention process (Alon et al., 2018). Professional development opportunities and cross-cultural experiences should be made an explicit part of career progression and lifelong development (Alon et al., 2018). Besides, periodic improvement workshops and cultural sensitivity training should target motivational, behavioral, or cognitive influence on communication skills, cultural awareness, teamwork, cooperation, and cohesiveness (Di Stefano, Cataldo, & Laghetti, 2019). Furthermore, companies need to incentivize diversity and link intercultural outcomes to other metrics as a strategic tactic to motivate learning, tolerance, sensitivity, and social mindfulness (Meng et al., 2017). Ongoing support, global resources, and collaborative partnerships are also required to bridge cultural differences, lessen multi-ethnic misunderstandings, and mitigate relational conflicts during the ambiguous and uncertain periods of change or transitions (Di Stefano et al., 2019; Le Sueur & Tapela, 2018; Vaccaro & Camba, 2018).

Conclusion

One of the notable realities of globalization, open-market trade, and advanced communicative technologies is culturally and geographically diverse workforce striving to achieve a common organizational goal. Despite the situational ambiguities and humanistic complexities resulting from such globalized interconnectedness and interdependence, corporations continue to seek new opportunities for financial growth and innovative advantage in cross-cultural settings worldwide. Therefore, organizations in the 21st-century business environment need globally competent and culturally intelligent leaders who are capable of functioning effectively across the globe. This chapter of *The Refractive Thinker®* underscores integrative insights into global leadership competencies like cultural intelligence, global mindset, emotional intelligence, as well as the fundamental components, such as awareness, mindfulness, and authentic leadership construct. The implication is to prepare leaders for the multidisciplinary competencies required to leverage global business strategies and inclusive engagement of culturally diverse stakeholders for successful business outcomes. Nonetheless, incumbent corporations are responsible for building the capabilities of their workforce and emerging leaders to increase viable possibilities beyond national and cultural boundaries. Through refractive thinking, it is discernable that thriving in a world of endless opportunities is contingent on how quickly and effectively organizations can leverage global leadership and cross-cultural competencies to match situational reality.

THOUGHTS FROM THE ACADEMIC ENTREPRENEUR

The problem to be solved:

- The resulting dynamics of globalization create situational ambiguities and humanistic complexities for global leaders.

The goals:

- Understanding the global and cross-cultural competencies that leaders need to succeed beyond national and cultural boundaries.

The questions to ask:

- What competencies do global leaders need to thrive in geographically and culturally diverse business environments?

- What are the workplace strategies for increasing cultural and global leadership competency?

Today's Business Application:

- Effective leaders who possess multidisciplinary competencies and aptitudes can better manage multicultural stakeholders and leverage interpersonal relationships for successful global outcomes.

- Global leaders need to be authentic and morally grounded, regardless of the geographical and cultural setting.

- Global operational success depends on how quickly and effectively leaders can integrate and adapt to culturally diverse business environments as situationally necessary.

REFERENCES

Ade, G., Majaro, T., & Poshi, M. (2019). *The Refractive Thinker® Vol XVI: Generations: Strategies for managing generations in the workforce: Chapter 8: Multigenerational leadership & engagement: A balancing act for 21st century leaders* (p. 151–163). Grayslake, IL: The Refractive Thinker® Press

Adewoye, A. (2013). Unique competencies required for female leadership success in the 21st century (Doctoral dissertation). Available from ProQuest Dissertations and Theses database. (UMI No. 3603342)

Alon, I., Boulanger, M., Elston, J. A., Galanaki, E., Martínez de Ibarreta, C., Meyers, J., & . . . Vélez?Calle, A. (2018). Business cultural intelligence quotient: A five?country study. *Thunderbird International Business Review, 6,* 237–250. doi:10.1002/tie.21826

Ang, S., & Van Dyne, L. (2015). Conceptualization of cultural intelligence: Definition, distinctiveness, and nomological network. In *Handbook of cultural intelligence: Theory, measurement, and applications,* (pp. 21–33). New York, NY: Routledge.

Azevedo, A., & Shane, M. J. (2019). A new training program in developing cultural intelligence can also improve innovative work behavior and resilience: A longitudinal pilot study of graduate students and professional employees. *The International Journal of Management Education, 17*(3), 100303. doi:10.1016/j.ijme.2019.05.004

Bartel-Radic, A., & Giannelloni, J.-L. (2017). A renewed perspective on the measurement of cross-cultural competence: An approach through personality traits and cross-cultural knowledge. *European Management Journal, 35,* 632–644. doi:10.1016/j.emj.2017.02.003

Bernardo, A. B. I., & Presbitero, A. (2018). Cognitive flexibility and cultural intelligence: Exploring the cognitive aspects of effective functioning in culturally diverse contexts. *International Journal of Intercultural Relations, 66,* 12–21. doi:10.1016/j.ijintrel.2018.06.001

Chai, D. S., Jeong, S., Kim, J., Kim, S., & Hamlin, R. G. (2016). Perceived managerial and leadership effectiveness in a Korean context: an indigenous qualitative study. *Asia Pacific Journal of Management, 3,* 789–820. doi: 10.1007/s1049.

Chandwani, R., Agrawal, N. M., & Kedia, B. L. (2016). Mindfulness: Nurturing global mind-set and leadership. *Thunderbird International Business Review, 58,* 617–625. doi:10.1002/tie.21760

Chao, M. M., Takeuchi, R., & Farh, J. L. (2017). Enhancing cultural intelligence: The roles of implicit culture beliefs and adjustment. *Personnel Psychology, 70*(1), 257–292. doi:10.1111/peps.12142

Daher, N. (2015). Emotional and cultural intelligences as an assessment tool for recruiting, selecting, and training individual candidates. *International Journal of Business & Public Administration, 12*(1), 167–180. Retrieved from http;//www. brainmass.com

D'Almeida, A., & Grossi, A. (2016). The *fascinating worlds of unconscious bias and developmental policy*. Retrieved from http://www.theguardian.com

Dalton, S., & Villagran, M. (2018). Minimizing and addressing implicit bias in the workplace: Be proactive, part one. *College & Research Libraries News, 79,* 478. doi:10.5860/crln.79.9.478

Darvishmotevali, M., Altinay, L., & De Vita, G. (2018). Emotional intelligence and creative performance: Looking through the lens of environmental uncertainty and cultural intelligence. *International Journal of Hospitality Management, 73,* 44–54. doi 10.1016/j.ijhm.2018.01.014

Di Stefano, G., Cataldo, E., & Laghetti, C. (2019). The client-oriented model of cultural competence in healthcare organizations. *International Journal of Healthcare Management, 12*(3), 189. doi:10.1080/20479700.2017.1389476

Dutton, K. (2018). Increasing diversity, awareness, and inclusion in corporate culture: Investigating communities of practice and resource groups among employees. *Development and Learning in Organizations: An International Journal, 32*(6), 19–21. doi:10.1108/DLO-11-2018-132

Fitzsimmons, S. R., Liao, Y., & Thomas, D. C. (2017). From crossing cultures to straddling them: An empirical examination of outcomes for multicultural employees. *Journal of International Business Studies, 48*(1), 63–89. doi:10.1057/s41267-016- 0053-9

Flynn, S. I. (2019). Technology in global markets. Salem press encyclopedia. Retrieved from http://www.salempress.com

Forsyth, B. (2015). Cultural intelligence and global leadership. *Journal of Leadership, Accountability & Ethics, 12*(2), 130–135. Retrieved from http://www. na-businesspress.com

Glasener, K. M., Martell, C. A., & Posselt, J. R. (2018). Framing diversity: Examining the place of race in institutional policy and practice post-affirmative action. *Journal of Diversity in Higher Education, 12*(1), 3–16. doi:10.1037/dhe0000086

Goleman, D., Boyatzis, R. E., & McKee, A. (2013). *Primal leadership: Unleashing the power of emotional intelligence*. Boston, MA: Harvard Business Press.

Gunkel, M., Schlaegel, C., & Taras, V. (2016). Cultural values, emotional intelligence, and conflict handling styles: A global study. *Journal of World Business, 51,* 568–585. doi:10.1016/j.jwb.2016.02.001

Heppner, W. L., & Kernis, M. H. (2007). "Quiet ego" functioning: The complementary roles of mindfulness, authenticity, and secure high self?esteem. *Psychological Inquiry, 18*(4), 248–251. Retrieved from http://www.jstor.org

Iheduru-Anderson, K. (2015). Cultural diversity & inclusivity. Where are we at?

Australian Nursing & Midwifery Journal, 23(4), 18–23. Retrieved from http://europepmc.org

Jaradat, M., & Iurian, S. D. (2019). Adapting leadership methods to global challenges: Interactive leadership. *Calitatea, 20,* 487. Retrieved from http://www.srac.ro

Jiang, F., Ananthram, S., & Li, J. (2018). Global mindset and entry mode decisions: Moderating roles of managers' decision-making style and managerial experience. *Management International Review (MIR), 58,* 413. doi:10.1007/s11575-018-0348-0

Johnson, A., & Jackson Williams, D. (2015). White racial identity, color-blind racial attitudes, and multicultural counseling competence. *Cultural Diversity & Ethnic Minority Psychology, 21,* 440–449. doi:10.1037/a0037533

Jordan, S. L., Ferris, G. R., & Lamont, B. T. (2019). A framework for understanding the effects of past experiences on justice expectations and perceptions of human resource inclusion practices. *Human Resource Management Review, 29,* 386–399. doi:10.1016/j.hrmr.2018.07.003

Jyoti, J., & Kour, S. (2017). Factors affecting cultural intelligence and its impact on job performance. *Personnel Review, 46,* 767–791. doi:10.1108/pr-12-2015-0313

Landesz, T. (2018). Authentic leadership and Machiavellianism in young global leadership. *The ISM Journal of International Business, 2*(2), 39–51. Retrieved from http://www.ism.edu

Lane, H. W., Maznevski, M. L., & Mendenhall, M. E. (2004). Globalization: Hercules meets Buddha. In H. W. Lane, M. Maznevski, M. E. Mendenhall, & J. McNett (Eds.), *The Blackwell handbook of global management: A guide to managing complexity* (pp. 3–25). Oxford, England: Blackwell.

Levy, O., Beechler, S., Taylor, S., & Boyacigiller, N. A. (2017). What we talk about when we talk about "global mindset": Managerial cognition in multinational corporations. *Journal of International Business Studies, 38,* 231–258. doi:10.1057/palgrave.jibs.8400265

Le Sueur, H. M., & Tapela, V. (2018). Conditions for coaching to contribute to the adjustment of black African professionals. *South African Journal of Human Resource Management, 16*(1), N.PAG. doi:10.4102/sajhrm.v16i0.946

Lima Neves, V. M., & Amélia Tomei, P. (2017). The effect of global mindset on leadership behavior: An analysis of a diversified sample of countries. *International Journal of Knowledge, Culture & Change in Organizations: Annual Review, (1),* 19–37. doi:10.18848/1447-9524/CGP/v17i01/19-37

Livermore, D., & Soon, A. N. G. (2015). *Leading with cultural intelligence: The real secret to success.* New York, NY: AMACOM.

Majaro, T. (2018). Effects of lack of workplace relationships on long-term care nurses (Doctoral dissertation). Available from ProQuest Dissertations and Theses database. (UMI No.10927998)

Mathews, J. (2016). Toward a conceptual model of global leadership. *IUP Journal of Organizational Behavior, 15*(2), 38. Retrieved from https://www.iupindia.in

Mendenhall, M. E., Osland, J. S., Bird, A., Oddou, G. R., Maznevski, M. L., Stevens, M. J., & Stahl, G. K. (2013). *Global leadership: Research, practice, and development* (2nd ed.). Abingdon, UK: Rutledge.

Meng, J., Reber, B. H., & Rogers, H. (2017). Managing millennial communication professionals: Connecting generation attributes, leadership development, and employee engagement. *Acta Prosperitatis, 8,* 68–83. Retrieved from http://www.turiba.lv/en

Mor-Barak, M., E. (2017). *Managing diversity: Toward a globally inclusive workplace* (Fourth Edition). Los Angeles, CA: SAGE Publications, Inc.

Ott, D. L., & Michailova, S. (2018). Cultural intelligence: A review and new research avenues. *International Journal of Management Reviews, 20*(1), 99–119. doi10.1111/ijmr.12118

Sebastian Reiche, B., Bird, A., Mendenhall, M. E., & Osland, J. S. (2017). Contextualizing leadership: a typology of global leadership roles. *Journal of International Business Studies, 48,* 552–572.

Tuleja, E. A. (2014). Developing cultural intelligence for global leadership through mindfulness. *Journal of Teaching in International Business, 25*(1), 5–24. doi: 10.1080/08975930.2014.881275

Turner, J. R., Baker, R., Schroeder, J., Johnson, K. R., & Chung, C.-H. (2019). The global leadership capacity wheel. *European Journal of Training and Development, 43*(1/2), 105–131. doi:10.1108/ejtd-07–2018–0061

Vaccaro, A., & Camba, K. M. J. (2018). Cultural competence and inclusivity in mentoring, coaching, and advising. *New Directions for Student Leadership, (158)*, 87–97. doi:10.1002/yd.20290

Varela, S. A. (2018). The influence of cultural intelligence on intercultural business negotiation. *International Journal of Business and Social Science, 9*(3). doi:10.30845/ijbss.v9n3p3

Villarreal, J. (2014). A call to define the moral variable of authentic leadership. *Allied Academies International Conference: Proceedings of the Academy of Strategic Management (ASM), 13*(1), 1–3. Retrieved from http://www.alliedacademies.org

Walker, J. L. (2018). Do methods matter in global leadership development? Testing the global leadership development ecosystem conceptual model. *Journal of Management Education, 42*(2), 239–264. doi:10.1177/1052562917734891

Young, C. A., Haffejee, B., & Corsun, D. L. (2018). Developing cultural intelligence and empathy through diversified mentoring relationships. *Journal of Management Education, 42,* 319–346. doi:10.1177/1052562917710687

About the Authors . . .

Dr. Gail Ade is an ICF credentialed & Board Certified Executive Leadership, Business & Career Coach. Through intentional engagement, She facilitates breakthrough coaching to empower executive leaders (current and emerging), small business owners, professionals, and entrepreneurs to achieve sustainable success. As a social change advocate, Dr. Gail also partners with organizations to advance diversity beyond representation.

Dr. Gail earned her Doctor of Business Administration (DBA) in Organizational Leadership, and Master of Business Administration (MBA) in Human Resource Management. She also holds a Ph.D. Bridge to Management in Leadership & Organizational Strategy, as well as a Graduate Certificate in Industrial & Organizational Psychology.

Dr. Gail is an active member of the Society for Human Resource Management (SHRM), International Coach Federation (ICF), National Society of Leadership & Success, and Society for Diversity.

To reach Dr. Gail Ade, please **e-mail:** dradegail@gmail.com

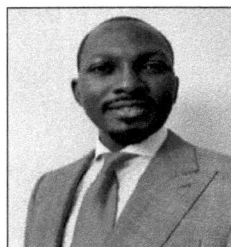

Dr. Tokunbo A. Majaro resides in the historic town of Ewing, NJ. Dr. Majaro holds several accredited degrees: a Master of Science (MS) in Healthcare Administration; and a Doctorate (Ph.D.) in Health Services-Public Health Policy from Walden University. His experience spans working on and managing clinical trials for biopharmaceutical companies with domestic and global operations. He is passionate about the success of organizational leaders. Dr. Tokunbo also provides professional coaching services to health care executives on effective leadership strategies.

Dr. Tokunbo is an active member of the American College of Healthcare Executives and the National Society of Leadership & Success.

To reach Dr. Tokunbo Majaro, please **e-mail:** drtmajaro@gmail.com

CHAPTER 8

Retaining New Teachers

Dr. Tammie L. Jones

Organizations regularly contend with employee turnover that is voluntary in nature. "More than 16,600 of special education teachers are expected to leave their occupation each year, on average, from 2016 to 2026, according to projections from the U.S. Bureau of Labor Statistics (Torpey, 2018, "Separations in Selected Chart 1")." The voluntary turnover rates continue to rise with current employees leaving their jobs early on in their career (Armache, 2014). Retaining employees is often difficult. Organizational leaders must be aware of the needs and concerns of their employees and create strategies to discover the reasons behind the voluntary turnover (Lewis, 2014). The objective for this chapter is to use refractive thinking to explore how leaders might retain their employees; in this case special education teachers.

A decrease in employee retention, particularly because of voluntary turnover, in the field of education can be significant (Jones, 2019). Retention encompasses important elements such as strategy seeking, goal-directed behaviors, rewards reinforcement, and performance-satisfaction (Laddha, Gabbad, & Gidwani, 2012). The retention and voluntary turnover rate among teachers in special education over teachers that teach general education in the United States remains to be a problem (Berry 2012; Major 2012).

Leadership can be a determinate of whether employees leave an organization ("How to Keep," 2015; Mills & Rose, 2011).

Leaders play a significant role in why employees leave; employees often leave not because of the organization itself, but the actual leaders (Mills & Rose, 2011). Employee voluntary turnover can affect everyone in the organization and lower morale (Thompson, 2014). The purpose of this chapter through the use of refractive thinking, is to address the retention of public-school teachers in special education teaching grades K-12 and the part that education leaders could possibly have in reducing voluntary turnover. The chapter focuses on schools in the United States. The problem that existed was teachers in special education are quitting their jobs, there is a deficit of teachers in special education in the United States (Vittek, 2015). To increase employee retention rates and reduce voluntary turnover, school leaders must examine their leadership styles and develop strategies that will retain teachers (Brandenburg, 2015).

Employee Retention 101

Historically employee retention was first studied by Fredrick Herzberg. Herzberg's (1959) theory was known as the theory of hygiene and motivation. The theory, also known as the dual-factor theory (Issa, 2016), included two factors: employment and motivation. The hygiene factor of the theory encompassed working circumstances and managerial circumstances (Lazaroiu, 2015). Lazaroiu (2015) also indicated that Herzberg affirmed that individuals have perceptions that involve work satisfaction or dissatisfaction. Herzberg wanted to know in the workplace setting, what satisfied or dissatisfied employees (Issa, 2016). Although Herzberg's hygiene factors included working environment, relationships with colleagues, and motivation, there are different factors in employee retention and work satisfaction. Responsibility, recognition, creativity, and innovation encouragement are factors in work satisfaction as well (Oke, Ajagbe, Ogbari, & Adeyeye, 2016).

Employees are assets to organizations. Retaining them is crucial. Employee turnover, to an organization, can be very costly. "The cost of replacing employees, who quit, ranges from 50% to 150 % of one year's salary" (Mosley & Irvine, 2015, p. 8). Effective leadership is one way that organizations could reduce employee retention and voluntary turnover (Jones, 2019). Leaders must be aware of the needs of employees, particularly new employees ("How to Keep," 2015). Increasing employee retention and reducing voluntary turnover consist require leaders to consider several factors. Some of the factors among the teachers include the level of job burnout, employee motivation, leadership support for their employees, and job satisfaction or dissatisfaction.

Factors Among the Teachers

Only a third of teachers leaving the profession are retirees (Westervelt, 2016). Approximately 15% or more leave their profession every year (Riggs, 2013). Turnover such as leaving the profession, going to other schools, or other factors are the highest rate among the teaching profession (Hughes, 2012). There are several things that may affect a decline in teacher retention. Burnout and stress, job satisfaction, motivation, and salaries are only some of the things that affect retention rates.

Burnout. Burnout can occur in any profession. Burnout can be a sense of mental fatigue (Larson & Vinberg, 2010). Maroney (2017) referenced a study in the Employee Engagement Series as stating "95 percent of human resource leaders say that employee burnout is sabotaging their workforce (para 2)." Some causes of burnout are stress, working long hours, and being run down because of large workloads (Maroney, 2017; Wall Street Journal, 2013). Unfortunately, when teachers feel burnout, it affects the students and others around them (Walker, 2016).

According to Zakrizevska (2015), teachers in special education, because of the capacity of caseloads, emotional and communication diversity among students, and physical well-being are susceptible to burnout. The complexities of their job requirements, the unsurmountable paperwork involved in maintaining state regulations requirements are also causing burnout (Zakrizevska, 2015). Job satisfaction could also be a factor.

Job Satisfaction. Job satisfaction contributes to job productivity (Abdullah & Akhar, 2016). Herzberg used words such as *satisfier* which he based on motivation and *dissatisfiers* which he based on hygiene (Abdullah & Akhar, 2016). To retain teachers in special education, like other employees, job satisfaction is very important (Jones, 2019). Leaders must utilize the job satisfiers to find ways to retain teachers. Yurchisin and Park (2010) mentioned two types of job satisfaction. Internal job satisfaction is the amount of emotional fulfillment that an employee feels about performing their job; extrinsic job satisfaction according to the two authors is the way an employee feels because of their compensation, rewards, job performance, and work relationships (Yurchisin & Park, 2010). When trying to increase retention rates and decrease voluntary turnover, motivating and maintaining motivated employees are other factors leaders need consider.

Motivation. What part does motivation play? Organizational commitment intensification will lead to improved retention rates among employees (Adams, Hester, Bradley, Myers, and Keating, 2014). Wilkie (2019, "Beware Technology and Competitors," para. 8) quoted Cord Himelstein, a Vice President of Marketing and Communication for an employee rewards and incentive company as stating "we know the two biggest reasons people leave their jobs is a lack of appreciation and a poor relationship with a direct manager." Motivation can help improve organizational performance. Motivation is more than just training and teaching employees. Leaders that understand the positive effects of motivation will have satisfied employees (Jones, 2019).

Lazaroiu (2015) contended, the attitudes of employees have an impact on their work attitudes. Lazaroiu also affirmed motivation goes directly to how an employee feels about their job, work performance, and environment. Motivating employees is important to balance the needs and wants of the company with those of the employee ("Motivation," 2014). As a form of support, leaders can motivate employees to stay in the organization. Employee's motivation increases from knowing that they're working towards a goal together (Carrison, 2014).

Salary. Teacher retention, like other professions, can be as simple as a salary increase. New teachers entering the profession, monetary influences are frequently a reason (Jones, 2019). According to Hutchinson (2015), teacher salaries are "25% less than professions such as marketing, nursing, and accounting" (p. 24). Joseph and Waymack (2014) contended that it takes up to 24 years for teachers to reach their *maximum* pay an estimate that most will probably not teach past 30 years. Although the cost of living adjustments are made, the teacher salaries are not enough (Joseph & Waymack, 2014). Salaries are important in job satisfaction for teachers (Oke, Ajagbe, Ogbari, & Adeyeye, 2016). Although money is a motivator, it is *not* the most important motivator (Hughes, 2012; Issa, 2016). Teachers, Hughes (2012) contended, like others in the workforce, evaluate all the benefits of the job.

Lack of Leader Support and Communication. Communication is beneficial in organizations. Communication is associated with quality leadership (Solaja et al., 2016). According to Jones (2019), open and clear communication between a teacher and a leader is essential in retaining new special education teachers. The ability to communicate effectively can help leaders identify and solve problems (Solaja et al., 2016). The idyllic leader always takes actions to support, foster the development and progress of his employees (Iqbal, 2015). Teachers in special education particularly new teachers, need support. By giving their employees the support needed, leaders have the ability to increase job loyalty.

Organizational leaders need to communicate with the school principals who in turn, should communicate with their teams and teachers. It is imperative to everyone involved to have complete knowledge of what is expected of them, as well as have an update of progress communicated. Communication amongst the teachers is also necessary. The teachers need to be able to give and receive feedback to each other. Communication and leadership support should not be options but major priorities instead.

The Leader's Roles in Retention

It is vital for leaders to comprehend the role an employee's attitudes have in organizational commitment. The topic of leadership has been discussed for decades. Schultz (2013), indicated that in collaboration with followers, and others, create results, and can envision future goals. Attitudes, relationships, and values of employees within an organization constitute organizational commitment (Apache, 2014). When leaders effectively focus on a retention strategy that includes implementing a culture in which employees want to stay, the organization will be successful (Ng'ethe, Namusonge, & Iravo, 2012).

Leader support can positively influence special education teachers and assist in their retention (Jones, 2019). Leadership has an impact on both job satisfaction and job dissatisfaction. Solaja, Idowu, and James (2016) believe there is a connection between a leader's style of communication and employee productivity. Education leaders demonstrating positive leadership performances can have a beneficial effect on educators (Mehdine-zhad & Mansouri, 2016).

Among employees, a leader's positive influence plays a crucial role (Jones, 2019). The support of organizational leaders is necessary. This support can come through various options. A lack of leader respect can be a cause of a decrease in the retention of teachers (Sturt, 2015). Things such as focusing on the positive impact of employee contributions can prove successful (Sturt, 2015). Inadequate leadership and a lack of administrator respect are additional reasons for low teacher retention (Oke1 et al., 2016).

Mentoring and Teacher Retention

Leadership support can come from the implementation of such programs as mentoring. Armache (2014) defined mentoring as the affiliation among the guide or mentor, novice, or mentee, offering support, guidance, and coaching is provided to the novice or mentee. In teacher retention, mentoring can be an asset. Mentoring makes a difference. According to Jones (2019) for a new special education teacher, a mentoring program can be pertinent to long-term development and extremely beneficial in increasing retention rates.

According to research, mentoring can be important in the first years of teaching (Jones, 2019). Mentoring helps new teachers work through potential problems, allows teachers to start the job with assistance from experienced teachers, and enhances professional growth and development (Dag and Sari, 2017). Prepared teachers leave their professions at a lower rate than non-prepared teachers (Westervelt, 2016). Very often employees, particularly new employees may require the extra support that a senior employee may be able to provide. Mentoring offers personal and professional direction to a new teacher (Dag and Sari, 2017).

Mentoring, professional development training and a positive impact of teamwork among teachers may demonstrate small achievements (Fisher, 2011). Mentoring employees as well as showing the employee recognition are ways to inspire success-fulness at work (Sturt, 2015). One-on-one mentoring will allow for feedback, support, and open communication. "A mentor would typically provide either formal, informal, or both, kinds of training and supervision to the protégé who the mentor believes will subsequently serve the organization capable" (Dow, 2014, p. 105). Early career teachers value the support that comes from mentoring programs (Jones, 2019).

Summary

Voluntary turnover among employees, greatly impacts orga-nizations and many organizations find retaining their employees difficult (Mushrush, 2015). An employer must know how to retain their employees (Laddha, Singh, Gabbad, & Gindwani, 2012). Leadership style has an impact on job retention and vol-untary turnover (Brandenburg, 2015). Leaders must be aware of the needs of employees, particularly new employees ("How to Keep", 2015). Retaining employees and reducing employee voluntary separation is crucial to education. An effective leader influences follower (Nanjundeswaraswamy & Swamy, 2014).

Leadership is about preparing the leader for anything that may arise within the business environment. The challenges that leaders face is often difficult to determine the best action to take. It is important for leaders to understand some of the reasons teach-ers in special education are leaving their professions. It is equally as important for leaders to then determine the steps necessary to retain those employees. According to Jones (2019) for a new special education teacher, a mentoring program can be pertinent to long-term development and extremely beneficial in increasing retention rates.

A decrease in employee retention, particularly due to voluntary turnover, in the field of education can be detrimental. Retention encompasses important elements such as the need, the seeking of strategies, goal-directed behavior, rewards reinforcement, and performance-satisfaction (Laddha, Gabbad, & Gidwani, 2012). Organizations regularly contend with employee turnover that is voluntary in nature. "The U.S. Bureau of Labor Statistics reports the average yearly voluntary turnover in all industries is close to 32%" (Magloff, 2015). According to Davis (2013), leadership, job satisfaction, communication, interaction, and motivation, are aspects that can assist in increasing employee retention and reducing voluntary turnover.

Refractive Thinking Recommendations

Leaders must have better communication with their employees. The leaders must realize that each employee does not respond the same way to the same type of communication (i.e. text messages). Leaders must realize that saying there is an open-door policy and implementing an open-door policy are two different things (Jones, 2019). Employees need support and leaders must support them when needed. Support can come from motivation, empowering, and validation. Leaders must develop and implement mentoring programs to help new employees. Leaders must develop strategies to increase employee commitment and organizational loyalty.

Very often employees, particularly new employees may require the extra support and time that a senior employee may be able to provide. New teachers must foster new relationships with other teachers for support (i.e. classroom assistance, questions, brainstorming, etc.). New teachers must take the initiative to ask for assistance from their leaders if needed.

Conclusion

A decrease in employee retention, particularly because of voluntary turnover, in the field of education can be significant (Jones, 2019). The purpose of this chapter through the use of refractive thinking, was to address the retention of public-school teachers in special education teaching grades K-12 and the part that education leaders could have in reducing voluntary turnover. The chapter focused on schools in the United States. The problem that exists was teachers in special education were quitting their jobs and there is a deficit of teachers in special education in the United States (Vittek, 2015).

The chapter was to use refractive thinking to explore how leaders might retain their employees; in this case special education teachers. Some of the factors that have impacted special education teachers were explored. The factors were burnout, motivation, leader communication with teachers, and leader support. Retaining employees and reducing employee voluntary separation is crucial to education. It is vital for leaders to comprehend the role an employee's attitudes have in organizational commitment. Attitudes, relationships, and values of employees within an organization constitute organizational commitment (Apache, 2014). Leaders make the difference on whether or not a special education teacher remain on their job (Jones, 2019).

THOUGHTS FROM THE ACADEMIC ENTREPRENEUR

The problem to be solved:

- Reducing employee voluntary turnover rates among new special education teachers
- Educational leaders developing and implementing strategies or programs for new special education teachers

The goals:

- To increase employee retention rates and reduce voluntary turnover, school leaders must examine their leadership styles and develop strategies that will retain teachers (Brandenburg, 2015).

The questions to ask:

- How can education leaders increase employee retention rates among new special education teachers?

Today's Business Application:

- Effective leaders who understand and the needs of new special education teachers can increase organization's retention rates.
- The impact of low workforce retention rates, high voluntary turnover, and the role that leaders play has great significance.
- Clear and open communication with the new special education teachers will help leaders
- Developing and implementing programs for new employees such as mentoring programs will help with retaining new special education teachers.

REFERENCES

Adams, K. M., Hester, P. T., Bradley, J. M., Meyers, T. J., & Keating, C. B. (2014). Systems theory as the foundation for understanding systems. *Systems Engineering, 17*(1), 112–123. doi:10.1002/sys.21255

Armache, J. (2014). Motivational factors effecting employees' retention and productivity. *Ethics & Critical Thinking Journal,* (3), 131–149. Retrieved from http://www.franklinpublishing.net

Berry, L. M. (1997). *Psychology at work.* San Francisco, CA: McGraw Hill Companies. Retrieved from http://www.businessdictionary.com/definition/motivation.html

Brandenburg, D. (2015, December). Employee turnover because of poor leadership. *Small Business—Chron.com.* Retrieved from http://smallbusiness.chron.com/employee-turnover-because-poor-leadership-24806.html

Dag, N., & Sari, M. H. (2017). Areas of mentoring needs of novice and preservice teachers. *International Electronic Journal of Elementary Education, 10*(1), 115–129. Retrieved from https://www.iejee.com/index.php/IEJEE/article/view/304

Davis, T. L. (2013, January 1). A qualitative study of the effects of employee retention on the organization. *ProQuest LLC.* Retrieved from https://eric.ed.gov/?id=ED552437

How to keep new hires on board, productive and engaged. (2015). *Manager's Legal Bulletin, 29*(12), 3. Retrieved from https://managerslegalbulletin.com/

Hughes, G. D. (2012). Teacher retention: Teacher characteristics, school characteristics, organizational characteristics, and teacher efficacy. *Journal of Educational Research, 105*(4), 245–255. Retrieved from https://www.tandfonline.com/doi/full/10.1080/00220671.2011.584922

Iqbal, S. (2015). Leadership: What it is, what it is not. *Pakistan Business Review, 17*(1), 201–206. https://dx.doi.org/http://journals.iobmresearch.com/index.php/PBR/issue/archive

Issa Eid, M. T. (2016). What do people want from their jobs?: A dual factor analysis based on gender differences. *Journal of Social & Economic Statistics, 5*(1), 42–55. Retrieved from http://www.jses.ase.ro/downloads/Vol5NO1/Issa-Eid.pdf

Jones, T. L. (2019). *Employee retention management and leadership of special education teachers: A narrative inquiry.* Retrieved from Dissertations & Theses @ University of Phoenix; ProQuest Dissertations & Theses Global. (UMI No. 13428568)

Joseph N., Waymack, N., & National Council on Teacher Quality. (2014). Smart money: What teachers make, how long it takes and what it buys them. *National Council on Teacher Quality.* Retrieved from https://www.nctq.org/publications/Smart-money:-What-teachers-make,-how-long-it-takes-and-what-it-buys-them

Laddha, A., Singh, R., Gabbad, H., & Gidwani, G. D. (2012). Employee retention: An art to reduce turnover. *International Journal of Management Research and Reviews, 2*(3), 453–458. Retrieved from https://pdfs.semanticscholar.org/97f9/7da2cfbd38a30d3d8ea822366eca4266d94a.pdf

Lazaroiu, G. (2015). Work motivation and organizational behavior. *Contemporary Readings in Law and Social Justice, 7*(2), 66–75. Retrieved from https://www.addletonacademicpublishers.com/search-in-crlsj/2657-work-motivation-and-organizational-behavior

Maroney, J, (2017, February 1). The top three factors driving employee burnout. *Forbes*. Retrieved from https://www.forbes.com/sites/groupthink/2017/02/01/the-biggest-workplace-challenge-employee-burnout/#3e7dc3803549

Mills, S., & Rose, J. (2011). Challenging behavior and burnout. *Journal of Intellectual Disability Research, 55*, 844–857. Retrieved from https://onlinelibrary.wiley.com/journal/13652788

Mushrush, W. (2015). Reducing employee turnover. *University of Missouri*. Retrieved from http://missouribusiness.net/article/reducing-employee-turnover/

Nanjundeswaraswamy, T. S., & Swamy, D. R. (2014). Leadership styles. *Advances in Management, 7*(2), 57–62. Retrieved from https://www.researchgate.net/publication/272509462_Leadership_styles

Ng'ethe, J. M., Namusonge, G. S., & Iravo, M. A. (2012). Influence of leadership style on academic staff retention in public universities in Kenya. *International Journal of Business and Social Science, 3*(21), 297–302. Retrieved from http://ijbssnet.com/journals/Vol_3_No_21_November_2012/31.pdf

Oke1, A. O., Ajagbe2, M. A., Ogbari3, M. E., & Adeyeye4, J. O. (2016). Teacher retention and attrition: A review of the literature. *Mediterranean Journal of Social Sciences, 7*(2) S1. doi:10.5901/miss.2016.v7n2s1p371

Riggs, L. (2013). Why do teachers quit and why do they stay? *The Atlantic*. Retrieved from https://www.theatlantic.com/education/archive/2013/10/why-do-teachers-quit/280699/

Solaja, O. M., Idowu, F. E., & James, A. E. (2016). Exploring the relationship between leadership communication style, personality trait and organizational productivity. *Serbian Journal of Management, 11*(1), 99–117. doi:10.5937/sjm11–8480

Sturt, D. (2015). The power of "thank you." *Training Journal, 57*. Retrieved from http://www.trainingjournal.com/search/site/D.%20Sturt

Tanner, R. (2015). Voluntary turnover: They usually leave their bosses, not their jobs. *Management is a Journey*. Retrieved from: http://managementisajourney.com/voluntary-turnover-they-usually-leave-their-bosses-not-their-jobs/

Torpey, E. (2018, October). Projections for teachers: How many are leaving the occupation? *United States Department of Labor Bureau of Labor Statistics*.

Retrieved from https://www.bls.gov/careeroutlook/2018/data-on-display/how-many-teachers-are-leaving.htm?view_full

Vittek, J. E. (2015). Promoting special educator teacher retention: A critical review of the literature. *SAGE Open.* https://dx.doi.org/10.1177/2158244015589994

WJS Wall Street Journal Podcast. (2017, February 28). *Employee burnout is getting worse.* Retrieved from http://www.wsj.com/podcasts/employee-burnout-is-getting-worse/C83341CD-08B4-4440-BFAE-0C9D884CF393.html

Wilkie, D. (2019, May 07). *Best and worst jobs unveiled, but can workers be happy even if stressed and underpaid?* Retrieved from https://www.shrm.org/resourcesandtools/hr-topics/employee-relations/pages/best-and-worst-jobs-2019.aspx

Zakrizevska, M. (2015). Professional burnout of special education teachers in Latvia. *Journal of Business Management, (9),* 169–534, 47–55. Retrieved from https://www.riseba.lv/en/research/publications/2015

About the Author . . .

Dr. Tammie L. Jones is from South Carolina. She has a BA in Psychology from Marymount University in Arlington, VA; with a Master's of Business Administration (MBA), as well as a Master's of Management Human Resource Management (MM/HRM) through University of Phoenix.

Being a military spouse allowed her to travel and live in various places. While in Springfield, VA, Dr. Tammie worked as a Special Education teacher for an alternative high school. In Hawaii, Dr. Tammie worked as the Coordinator for the Goodwill Industries of Hawaii Adult Day Health Program. At Easter Seals of Hawaii, she was a Case Manager for both adults and children with physical and intellectual disabilities.

She is an active member of the American Management Association (AMA) and a volunteer for the Special Olympics.

Dr. Tammie is a published author; her dissertation is entitled *Employee Retention Management and Leadership of Special Education Teachers: A Narrative Inquiry.*

Interests include the business management field and leadership. Her hobbies include research, writing, reading, and knitting.

To reach Dr Tammie L. Jones, **email:** tammie-jones@hotmail.com or **LinkedIn:** https://www.linkedin.com/in/dr-tammie-l-jones-9054591b

CHAPTER 9

The Hidden DNA
that Impacts Culture

Dr. Dawn Marie Kier

A Gallup study (2019) indicated that 50% of all hires will turn over in 18 months and in the fast-casual industry. The term fast casual refers to a type of food establishment whereby a mix of fast service in a sit-down environment with the promise of higher food quality exists (Fast Casual, 2015). Full table service is not offered in fast casual and some fast-casual establishments even have a drive through; however, the food quality remains higher than that of a traditional fast food establishment (Fast Casual, 2015). The reality is that employers can screen, assess, test, interview, and give walk throughs, but until they have people working in healthy environments, eventually what is on the inside of the employee is going to come out. Healthy environments are known by reduced turnover, higher levels of employee engagement and strong workplace retention. Organizations see it come out in terms of friction that occurs with customer interactions or how employees show up in response to their team or direct supervisor.

We all come to work with our hurts, habits and our *hang ups*. How do employers overcome these hurts, habits, and hang ups that their people bring with them to work so that when they are at work, they can be effective, efficient, productive, and ultimately beneficial to all the people they serve? The answer can be found in organizational health, the innermost part of an organization's culture. Healthy people enable healthy workplaces, and the reverse of that statement is true. Why should you care? The cost to employers in the United States in loss productivity and engagement is $550B. The refractive thinking suggests that there is a clear link between the environments that are created, the employees who work in them, and the leaders who lead them.

Turnover remains at 50% in the United States and organizations state culture as one of the differentiating factors in retaining talent and engaging the workforce. According to Gallup (2018), 70% of all employees remain disengaged. In summary, only one third of most teams are engaged, and of the one third, 3 out of 10 employees actively seek other opportunities. The workplace is in trouble! A strong culture, whereby retention and engagement exceed the 35% United States norm is attractive quality for applicants (Porter, 2013). In the fast casual and fast food industry, Chick-Fil-A is the leader known for its culture and corresponding employee commitment. Brands that seek to emulate the culture have a direct effect on employee commitment and engagement (Ortega-Parra & Ángel Sastre-Castillo, 2013).

Organizations invest sizable resources in recruiting, selecting, onboarding, training, and retaining employees (Kier, 2017). Having a winning culture that promotes growth and employee retention remains the pinnacle challenge in maintaining a competitive advantage in business (Mony, 2014). A winning culture includes positive employee engagement, organizational trust, and committed employees who are passionate about living the organization's values and achieving the organization's mission (Rogers & Meehan, 2007). High-performing, winning cultures have been known to contribute to increased profitability, greater than average returns, and increased engagement and performance (Laks, 2008). Culture and values arguably position organizations as an employer of choice. Moreover, some employees make employment decisions, whether to stay or leave, based on the lived culture versus the stated values (Porter, 2013). A large reason why employees join an organization is because of their opportunities and values associated with the brand. Senior leaders are responsible for upholding the values and making decisions consistent with those values. When organizations failed to strike a balance between what they say and what they do, organizational discontentment occurs (Kier, 2017).

Ultimately, leaders shape the culture and maintain its architecture (Schein, 2010). Executives and officers of the company guide the organization's unspoken behavior and rules of operation (Kier, 2017). The guidelines and behaviors, known as organizational culture, dictate how employees, as well as consumers and vendors who engage with the brand, should behave (Mosley, 2014; McLaren, 2011). Loyal customers support brands that they believe in; likewise, employees engage and support brands that they believe in. Therefore, values congruency and cultural alignment must exist for employees in organizations to operate harmoniously.

Lencioni's (2012) research in the book, *The Advantage,* indicated that organizational culture, independent of the industry, remains the competitive advantage in the marketplace. Research indicated that employees can become discontent when they learn that the organization's operating practices vary from the espoused values (Kier, 2017; Porter, 2013). Researchers have looked for clues in the organizational environment that explain the tension that leaders experience between their espoused values and the organization's practices, but the organizational triggers that cause leaders to act in direct opposition to their espoused values or the organization's policies and practices have limited research (Moreno, 2011). Moreover, current research and organizations such as Glass Door cite that employees make decisions to leave organizations when they discover a mismatch between espoused values and perceived values (Kier, 2017; Moreno, 2011; Porter,

2013). The winning cultures that leaders seek to create are often derailed when words and actions do not align (Moreno, 2011).

In an industry where turnover is high and where the cost of retraining one employee is 6 to 9 months of that employee's salary, employee retention remains a key component of maintaining a competitive edge (Chronicle, 2016). Organizations make many efforts to sell future employees on the culture of the organization in efforts to lure the potential employees to the organization (Simoneaux & Stroud, 2014). In contrast, a silent expectation of employees is that the senior leaders would deliberately align, and lead consistently, with the organization's state culture. In contrast, employees (Simoneaux & Stroud, 2014).

Experts often cite culture as a contributing reason as to why businesses succeed or fail, yet little literature exits on the senior leader's role in the success or failure of an organization based upon values (Kaarst-Brown, Nicholson, von Dran, & Stanton, 2004; Thornbury, 2003). The tone of the organization, as set by the executive level leaders in the organization, impacts everything and every area of the organization, whether conscious or unconscious (Shapiro & Naughton, 2015). Because culture is more than an identity, the messages that come from the actual practices reinforce norms and acceptable standards of operations (Mankins, 2013). When a discrepancy between what is said and what is done occurs, uncertainty exists (Hatch & Schultz, 2001). A dichotomy between the articulated culture and the enacted lived culture of an organization can cause angst and uncertainty by employees and senior leaders alike (Kier, 2017; McCuddy & Nondorf, 2008). When organizations failed to strike a balance between what they say and what they do, organizational discontentment occurs, begging to question the authenticity of the leader and the instituted culture (Kier, 2017).

In the fast-casual industry in which turnover for a $10/hr employee exceeds $3000, and the cost retraining that employee exceeds $9,000, employee retention remains a pinnacle of competitive advantage and organizational success (Gallup, 2018; Jonsen, Galunic, Weeks, & Braga, 2015). Employers make many efforts to attract employees to an organization, and that typically happens through an expression and selling of the organization's culture (Jonsen et al., 2015). To keep an employee within an organization, a silent expectation is that all individuals, especially the senior leaders, would deliberately align with and live out the stated organizational culture (Kier, 2017).

Employees hold their leaders in high esteem and look to emulate their practices both seen and unseen (Klein, 2004; Northouse, 2009). The senior leaders in turn have a high responsibility to provide consistent framework; however, senior leaders are not able to do so 100% of the time (Klein, 2004; Northouse, 2009). Several things could occur when employees learn that their senior leaders do not espouse the company values, nor do they live out the stated organizational culture. "First, the employees can become disengaged. Second, the employers give their employees the permission to negate accepted behavior in the organization. Third, employees could be disappointed to the point where they leave the organization as they become disenchanted with senior leaders" (Kier, 2017, p. 4).

Employees feel a sense of entitlement because they expect the senior leaders to *walk the walk and talk the talk* (Kier, 2017; Moreno, 2011). In most instances, the leader carries out the vision, the strategic pillars, and the stated values; however, some more difficult decisions can cause a leader to misalign with the stated values versus the lived values. When lower-level employees witness senior leaders making decisions and carrying out actions that blatantly defy the stated organizational culture, employee harm occurs (Porter, 2013; Boyd & Begley, 2002). The harm is recognized as employee turnover, employee disengagement, and lack of trust in leadership. At times, the lasting effects of this organizational harm are irreparable. The $550 billion engagement issue is representative of the lack of congruency and consistency between what is said and done in organizations. Because employees hold their leaders in a higher esteem, the senior leaders bear the brunt and ownership of this phenomenon.

Research indicated reasons why employees fail to assimilate within a given culture (Hatch & Schultz, 2001). Organizations look for a strong candidate fit with its employees. Part of this fit remains the personal values of the candidate. A misfit can happen when the employee's values do not align with the organization's values (Kier, 2017). Literature references that employees become disgruntled and ultimately decide to leave organizations when there is a mismatch between espoused values and the employees' culture that was experienced in the workplace (Kier, 2017; Porter, 2013). There are instances where the senior leaders' words and actions regarding values and the state of culture misalign (Buckner, 2002). Misalignment between stated and enacted values and culture is a matter of heavy research from the viewpoint of the employee; yet, few studies examine the phenomenon from the viewpoint of the senior leader (Jonsen et al., 2015). A gap in the literature requiring further investigation is the lack of data needed to understand the senior leaders who create the values which enable the culture and sometimes fail to live up to the very values that they create (Buckner, 2002; Moreno, 2011; Porter, 2013). Through their study, these researchers sought to understand the conditions that exist when senior leaders make decisions or have behaviors that are contrary to the culture and values that they state.

Employees hold their leaders in high esteem and look to emulate their practices both seen and unseen (Klein, 2004; Northouse, 2009). Organizational culture is the silent underpinning of what is felt and often not discerned in an organization (Baumgartner, 2009; Cameron & Quinn, 2011; Schein, 2010; Wilson, 2001).

The culture of an organization is essential to executives because it guides the way the executives lead and the decisions they make, visible and invisible (Popa, 2013). The leaders' unspoken behaviors and rules communicate what the organization truly values. Actualization of values occur during the intentional use of values to drive alignment between what is said and what is done (Ledbetter, 2005).

One component of organizational culture is espoused values. Espoused values are values that an organization asserts and hopes to live up to (Kier, 2017). Literature references the need to examine coping with and reconciling the mismatch between the stated espoused values and culture, lived culture and senior leader involvement (Ledbetter, 2005; Porter, 2013). Literature references that employees become disgruntled and ultimately decide to leave organizations when there is a mismatch between espoused values and the culture employees experienced in the workplace (Porter, 2013). When employees become disengaged with the business, the end results could be lack of performance, lack of productivity, voluntary separation, or overall lack of engagement (Porter, 2013). Because senior leaders are responsible for creating and shaping the environment, they are also responsible for aligning with the very environment they set (Magruder, 2008; Mosley, 2014). Distress occurs when what leaders say and do, do not align (Porter, 2013). Employees look for their leaders to be transparent and congruent with how they live out the rules that they have set for the entire organization (Boyd & Begley, 2002). When there is a disparity between what leaders say and what leaders do, employees tend to become disengaged with the business because high expectations are placed on the leaders *walk the walk and talk the talk* (Moreno, 2011; Sorenson 2005). The crux between what is seen, what is felt, and how organizations actually behave impacts the unseen basic underlying assumptions of an organization's culture (Kier, 2017). Recent research details organizational triggers that cause leaders to act in direct opposition to their espoused values or the organization's policies and practices (Kier, 2017; Moreno, 2011).

Acquiescent DNA

Kier (2017) studied 8 senior leaders in the Southeast, specifically in the fast-casual industry. The study revealed that senior leaders lacked enthusiasm about carrying out or watching certain employment decisions take place, yet they quietly gave their consent as to comply with the decision that caused the mismatch between espoused values and their lived organization's culture. That behavior is described as acquiescent DNA. Acquiesce refers to giving consent or agreeing quietly. DNA is a substance that carries genetic information in the cells of plants and animals. In this study, the most significant learning was that the DNA present in senior leaders when the mismatch of espoused values and the lived organization's culture is placated by acquiescent behavior. Acquiescent DNA is the term used to describe the phenomenon when leaders don't *walk the walk and talk the talk.*

Acquiescent DNA is a strand found in leaders that cause them to reluctantly acquiesce to employment decisions in the organizations that go against their values and culture (Kier, 2017). "While the leader does not intend to violate the values and culture, the employment decisions that are made challenge the leader personally, therefore, they acquiesce when they experience various pressure points including: exclusionary outcast, organizational pressure, limited authority, and perceived loss" (Kier, 2017, p. 88).

Being an exclusionary outcast, or fear of not being included, remained a key concerned of senior leaders studied. This loss is associated with loss of positional significance at the senior level. When leaders do not acquiesce to the decision then they are targeted as *not being aligned* or *not being on board.* This type of pressure caused the senior leaders in this study to go along with employment decisions that they knew would cause a mismatch in the espoused stated values and their lived organization's culture. Senior leaders avoid actions that give rise to the feeling of personal harm, in terms of loss of acceptance or loss of employment. When the mismatch occurred, 50% of the senior leaders questioned if they were being effective in their role, since they could not prevent the mismatch. Senior leaders also questioned if they should remain employed with their current organization or if they should seek employment elsewhere.

Senior leaders struggled with organizational pressure, or the fear of timing. Participants stated that there is no perfect scenario where the values can be lived out 100% of the time. In this instance, values and culture are violated because the negative effects of carrying out a termination decision is greater than the effects of retaining the individual in question. Many operational pressures are present, so when senior leaders are faced with dilemmas, tension can arise between espoused values and the pressures of the business.

Senior leaders felt they had limited authority therefore fearing other leaders at the senior level. Research affirms that senior leaders are part of a subculture; yet, the senior leaders are still employees. The senior leaders felt as though they did not have the power or the authority to veto decisions that were made by the Chief Executive Officer (CEO). This significant fact is often overlooked when examining how senior leaders feel and respond to pressure from their boss. Senior leaders did not always have the power to overturn decisions that were made that were inconsistent with the environment or culture that was set, and their personal values. They also feared that if they opposed the decision then they would be in jeopardy as well. One participant stated that in many ways, he felt no different than a 27-year-old who did not have wherewithal to confront situations that are wrong.

These senior leaders also carried a constant weight of perceived loss and the fear of losing their job. This study indicated that the senior leaders fear the repercussions associated with fighting for employment decisions they know are right. They fear loss of employment, status, and isolation for vocalizing their discontent. They also lacked the confidence or desire to *fall on the sword* for the employee in which the decision was being made (Kier, 2017).

Kier (2017) found a thread of Acquiescent DNA in an alarming 6 out of the 8 leaders studied. While countercultural, and while blatantly opposing of their beliefs about the decisions, this thread of acquiescent behavior exists in the actions of the senior leaders in the study. Noteworthy of mention remains that Acquiescent DNA does not reveal itself in the genesis of values creation nor does it show up in routine daily leadership tasks. Specifically, Acquiescent DNA lies dormant in the leader until the leader is placed in a situation where he or she does not agree with an employment decision the senior leader knows will cause incongruence in *walking the walk and talking the talk,* yet he or she reluctantly submits to the decision (Kier, 2017). The reasons why leaders acquiesce vary, and at times, the decision to acquiesce is for the good of the company, yet to the detriment to the employees. More research is required to determine if, like human DNA, mutation is possible to modify the behaviors associated with acquiescent DNA.

Conclusion

The behaviors associated with Acquiescent DNA include the inability to give feedback and the pressures associated with organizations and senior leaders failing to *walk the walk and talk the talk.* The results of Acquiescent DNA negatively impact an organization's culture and ultimately employee engagement. There is a plethora of information and data available to the organization.

Organizations conduct engagement surveys at rapid rates, yet, the rate of change anticipated from engagement surveys remains lacking. Most employees have the expectation that there will be positive change because of participating in an engagement survey. When employees participate by giving feedback and then the organization sits on it, they become even more disengaged because they feel like they participated all for not (Werman et al., 2019).

The reality is that in spite of all of the leadership training and coaching that we have received, it is still difficult to look a person who we have worked with in the whites of his or her eyes and give him or her feedback that is truthful, and in some cases painful. In our personal lives, husbands and wives have difficulty giving honest feedback of their concern with what the other person will think. How much more so in the workplace? As senior leaders evolve and as the science of happiness and gratitude enter into the workplace, there is a higher expectation for leaders to be eloquent when delivering feedback that is less than positive and to be able to give constructive criticism in a way that still honors the person and that is in line with the values of the organization. An implication for senior leaders would be to become aware of situations where their leadership ability can be called into question because they acquiesced to a decision on people in which they did not agree. Painfully difficult? Yes! Very few senior leaders have mastered that art of communication as found in Kier's (2017) study of senior leaders and the impact of Acquiescent DNA on culture.

The lack of mastery in the area of giving feedback creates the Acquiescent DNA strand. The inability to have difficult conversations well is what causes seemingly strong leaders, especially at the C suite level, to acquiesce to the very values and culture they put in place throughout the organization. In learning how to have these difficult conversations in a way that gives the employees the same value, same honor, and same respect as when they were hired, is a goal that we have yet to achieve, but it is possible. Through our consulting in the fast casual, healthcare, and retail industries, New Dawn found that giving leaders both the Head Work and the Heart Work needed to have these conversations allows them to hold true to the North Star they create for their organization. This changes engagement one person at a time, one heart at a time, one organization at a time.

A consulting client, who is a senior leader at his organization, went through several transitions and moved to various departments in the organization. He is part of an organization that is known for their culture and living out their values. He made some career limiting decisions based on the negative treatment he experienced from leaders earlier on in the organization. He is frustrated because he feels as if his career is limited and feels as employment decisions were made that were not done in the culture that he expected. While this senior leader is not actively disengaged to the naked eye, internally he is still harboring feelings of discontentment, resentment, and lack of value.

This acquiescent DNA continues to be a silent strand, active in producing harmful results in the bodies of organizations. In many cases, when organizations understand this thread is present or that acquiescent DNA affects their leaders or employees, the emphatics is to do nothing and to say, "that is their problem, they need to work through it." However, truly cultured centered organizations, more importantly the leaders who lead these organizations, will look at the overall health of the organization. These leaders know that each person who makes up the body of the organization affects their health, so they must courageously address it.

According to Gallup (2015), the manager alone accounts for 70% of the variance in team engagement based on: (a) a manager's innate tendencies, (b) a manager's engagement, and (c) an employee's perception of the manager's behavior. Thirty seven percent of all absenteeism, 72% of engagement, 60% of stress, and 50% of productivity are all tied to the manager (Gallup, 2019). Therefore, it remains critical for leaders and organizations to evaluate their health and to drive performance through the culture and values that they espouse. Leaders drive organizational culture, the organization's culture drives employee engagement, and employee engagement drives productivity and results. Identifying areas where Acquiescent DNA prevails in an organization can lead to discovering where misalignment and disengagement exists. From there, organizations have a chance at regaining its health by sustaining long-term performance and growth.

As a practical matter, New Dawn observed that the real struggle is that there is a growing number of employees at all levels in the organization who struggle with the silent undercurrent that is affecting their culture (Kier, 2017; Valentin, Valentin, & Nafukho, 2015). More awards are being given for *best places to work* and *top cultures;* however, in sight of these amazing organizations, the silent majority, according to research, are still disengaged in spite of what the public rewards say. Employees closest to the problem at the senior leadership team are aware of it and they see it in their engagement results. The question then becomes, *"how do we reengage the workforce and address what's happening deep within the iceberg?"* The iceberg of organizational culture model depicts that at the top are the things that we see. In the middle are the things that we think, but at the bottom are the things that we really feel. The things felt are deeply held beliefs. These beliefs are usually told employee to employee, senior leader to senior leader, and told around the water cooler or in times of great change. Unfortunately, these stories that harden underneath the organization's surface affect the way companies perform, how their leaders show up, and the heart behind which they navigate change, innovation, and growth.

The widespread dissonance continues to occur at multiple levels in organizations. This dissonance is centered around people, organizational alignment, leadership influence, as well as numbers related to culture, engagement, turnover, and retention. To accurately paint the picture, 3 out of 10 employees who remain are strong performers. Without a reallocation of talent and resources, and without a deliberate focus on the underpinnings that negatively impact organizational culture, the weight of the dissonance becomes a source of pain for the leader.

Three recommendations that organizations can implement to immediate impact their culture and Acquiescent DNA include: bold and radically transparent conversations with leaders, their teams, and employees alike. Organizations should identify and examine the bad actors that promulgate mismatches in the culture, and who lead by fear. Moreover, organizations should create a plan to acknowledge the inconsistent behaviors exhibited the bad actors and enlist a coach or training to support the employee with their gaps (Longenecker & Insch, 2018). Next, organizations should explore crucial conversations as a vehicle to help leaders and employees change their narrative and the story in an organization. The ability to have crucial conversations helps to address the conflict present between *walking the walk and talking the talk* (Delisle et al., 2016). Chief People Officers or Talent Management teams should conduct a townhall meeting *unplugged* to hear the stories of the employees who feel as though the leaders are doing one thing and saying another. The Chief People Officer and Talent Management teams must create a non-retaliatory environment for honest conversations and feedback to occur (Werman et al., 2019). Noteworthy of mention is that 80% of the senior leaders studied had some form of AD in their leadership. What is more, coaching and consulting clients recognize the AD behaviors in their environments. Applying intentional focus on the leaders who impact and influence the culture enables organizations to fight Acquiescent DNA and strengthen the negative perceptions of employees.

THOUGHTS FROM THE ACADEMIC ENTREPRENEUR

The problem to be solved:

- Preparing leaders to walk the walk and talk the talk when leading individuals, teams, and their organization.

- In spite of best efforts by managers and employees alike, there is a delta in communication that prevents real time feedback in a way that honors and values the person. The result of the gap is disengagement and substandard performance.

The goals:

- Increase retention and reduce turnover by driving engagement throughout multiple levels in an organization.

The questions to ask:

- Where is the organization vulnerable due to leadership not walking the walk and talking the talk?

- What are the silent areas in the organization's culture that are making the most noise and causing turnover?

Today's Business Application:

- Leaders who drive results through performance and effective communication can directly impact the disengaged workforce.

- A culture aligned with people, values, and leadership allows employees to contribute their best at all levels, while driving peak performance in a changing environment.

REFERENCES

Baumgartner, R. J. (2009). Organizational culture and leadership: Preconditions for the development of a sustainable corporation. *Sustainable Development, 17*(2), 102–113. doi:10.1002/sd.405

Boyd, D. P., & Begley, T. M. (2002). Moving corporate culture beyond the executive suite. *Corporate Governance: The International Journal of Business in Society, 2*(1), 13–20. doi:10.1108/14720700210418670

Cameron, K. S., & Quinn, R. E. (2011). *Diagnosing and changing organizational culture: Based on the competing values framework.* Reading, MA: Jossey Bass.

Delisle, M., Grymonpre, R., Whitley, R., & Wirtzfeld, D. (2016). Crucial conversations: an interprofessional learning opportunity for senior healthcare students. *Journal of Interprofessional Care, 30,* 777–786, doi:10.1080/13561820.2016.12 15971

Giberson, T. R., Resick, C. J., Dickson, M. W., Mitchelson, J. K., Randall, K. R., & Clark, M. A. (2009). Leadership and organizational culture: Linking CEO characteristics to cultural values. *Journal of Business and Psychology, 24*(2), 123–137. doi:10.1007/s10869-009-9109-1

Hatch, M. J., & Schultz, M. (2001). Are the strategic stars aligned for your corporate brand? *Harvard Business Review, 79*(2), 128–134. Retrieved from https://hbr.org/

Jonsen, K., Galunic, C., Weeks, J., & Braga, T. (2015). Evaluating espoused values: does articulating values pay off? *European Management Journal, 33,* 332–340. doi:10.1016/j.emj.2015.03.005

Kaarst-Brown, M., Nicholson, S., von Dran, G. M., & Stanton, J. M. (2004). Organizational cultures of libraries as a strategic resource. *Library Trends, 53*(1), 33–53. Retrieved from https://www.press.jhu.edu/journals/library-trends

Kier, D. M. (2017) *Senior leaders' connection in the mismatch between espoused values and their organizations' lived culture* (Unpublished doctoral dissertation). Argosy University, Atlanta, Georgia.

Klein, J. S. (2004). Corporate cultures: Why values matter. *Folio, 33*(12), 23. Retrieved from https://www.foliomag.com/

Laks, A. G. (2008). *Organizational culture transformation and leadership: experiences in a local government entity* (Doctoral dissertation). oAvailable from ProQuest Dissertations & Theses Global. (UMI No. 304822754)

Ledbetter, B. L. (2005). *Exploring the intersection of values and leadership for women executives in the for-profit sector* (Doctoral dissertation). Available from ProQuest Dissertations & Theses Global. (305360667).

Lencioni, P. (2012). *The advantage.* San Francisco, CA: Josey-Bass.

Longenecker, C., & Insch, G. S. (2018). Senior leaders' strategic role in leadership development. *Strategic HR Review, 17*(3), 143–149. doi:10.1108/SHR-02-2018-0014

Magruder, M. (2008). *A phenomenological study: Information technology executive leadership's influence on organizational culture* (Doctoral dissertation). Available from ProQuest Dissertations & Theses Global. (UMI: No. 1283124628)

Mankins, M. C. (2013). The defining elements of a winning culture. *Harvard Business Review.* Retrieved from https://hbr.org/2013/12/the-definitive-elements-of-a-winning-culture/

McCuddy, M. K., & Nondorf, J. G. (2009). Ethics in college and university admissions: A trilogy of concerns and arguments. *The International Journal of Educational Management, 23,* 537–552. doi:10.1108/09513540910990780

McLaren, J. P. (2011). *Mind the gap: Exploring congruence between the espoused and experienced employer brand* (Doctoral dissertation. An unpublished Dissertation Thesis, University of Pennsylvania, October).

Mony, P. (2014). *Values-based leadership in a healthcare organization: Its impact on decision making and organizational outcomes* (Doctoral dissertation). Available from ProQuest Dissertations & Theses Global. (UMI No. 1547942115)

Moreno, M. C. (2011). *Ethical dilemmas: Pressures on leaders to walk the talk* (Doctoral dissertation). Available from ProQuest Dissertations & Theses Global. (UMI No. 879040729)

Mosley, P. A. (2014). Engaging leadership: Knowing when to disengage. *Library Leadership & Management, 28*(4).

Northouse, P. G. (2009). *Leadership: Theory and practice* (5th ed.). Thousand Oaks, CA: Sage.

Ortega-Parra, A., & Ángel Sastre-Castillo, M. (2013). Impact of perceived corporate culture on organizational commitment. *Management Decision, 51,* 1071–1083. doi:10.1108/MD-08-2012-0599

Popa, B. M. (2013). Risks resulting from the discrepancy between organizational culture and leadership. *Journal of Defense Resources Management, 4*(1), 179–182. Retrieved from https://doaj.org/

Porter, T. J. (2013). Employees' responses to the mismatch between organizations' espoused values and basic assumptions about organizational culture (Doctoral dissertation). Available from ProQuest Dissertations & Theses Global. (UMI No. 1429763552)

Rogers, P., & Meehan, P. (2007). Building a winning culture. *Business Strategy Series, 8*(4), 254–261. doi:10.1108/17515630710684420

Schein, E. H. (2010). *Organizational culture and leadership* (Vol. 2). Hoboken, NJ: Wiley & Sons. doi:10.1108/17515630710684420

Shapiro, B., & Naughton, M. (2015). The expression of espoused humanizing values in organizational practice: A conceptual framework and case study. *Journal of Business Ethics, 126*(1), 65–81. doi:10.1007/s10551–013–1990-x

Simoneaux, S. L., & Stroud, C. L. (2014). Business best practices: A strong corporate culture is key to success. *Journal of Pension Benefits, 22*(1), 51–53. Retrieved from http://www.aspenpublishers.com

Sorenson, K. D. (2005). *Individual awareness and management of multiple value sets in the workplace* (Doctoral dissertation). Available from ProQuest Dissertations & Theses Global. (UMI No. 305430899)

Thornbury, J. (2003). Creating a living culture: The challenges for business leaders. *Corporate Governance, 3*(2), 68. doi:10.1108/14720700310474073

Valentin, M. A., Valentin, C. C., & Nafukho, F. M., (2015). The engagement continuum model using corporate social responsibility as an intervention for sustained employee engagement. *European Journal of Training and Development, 39*(3), 182–202. doi:10.1108/EJTD-01–2014–0007

Werman, A., Adlparvar, F., Horowitz J. K., & Hasegawa, M. O. (2019). Difficult conversations in a school of social work: exploring student and faculty perceptions. *Journal of Social Work Education, 55*(2), 251–264, doi:10.1080/1043779 7.2018.1520665

Wilson, A. M. (2001). Understanding organizational culture and the implications for corporate marketing. *European Journal of Marketing, 35*(3/4), 353–367. doi:10.1108/03090560110382066

About the Author . . .

Dr. Dawn Kier began her leadership journey almost as soon as she started her work history. She had 20 years of leadership experience before deciding to pursue her Doctorate in Organizational Leadership. Dr. Dawn started her own company in 2009, New Dawn Consulting. Since then, the company has grown and been shaped into what it is now: an organizational health firm. Dr. Dawn now has an additional meaning. Her friends and colleagues recognize Dr. Dawn not only as a holder of a doctorate, but also as a true "heart doctor." She is passionate about doing what is rarely spoken about, by recognizing the whole person within the workplace. Dr. Dawn brings with her an innate sense of wisdom and insight to each interaction. She has worked with global brands, diverse organizations, franchisees, leadership teams, and individuals. Her mission is to foster healthy cultures and healthy lives in the franchise, fast-casual, retail, healthcare, and non-profit space. She is a licensed minister and a native-born Californian. She and her family relocated to Historic Downtown Norcross where they currently reside.

To reach Dr. Dawn Marie Kier for information on organizational culture/values, change management, talent strategy, Acquiescent DNA, Team "Heart Work", or guest speaking, please visit her company **website:** http://www.newdawnconsulting.com **or e-mail:** dawn@consultingnewdawn.com

Why Can't Professional Educators Talk About the Elephants in the Room? The Undiscussables of Culture

Dr. Yvonne L. Gonzalez, Dr. Teresa Sanders & Dr. Cheryl Lentz

Why can't we talk about the elephants in the room? Think about the implications of not only *what* is said but by whom. Socially, there seems to be a particularly fiery response when White people make racial missteps involving Black people. Concurrently, when Black people make missteps involving White people, the term *reversed racism* (as opposed to simply *racism*) is employed.

Among Latino populations, political hot buttons, such as immigration control and border safety, created moving targets for those for and against these issues for their political value rather than the needs of the human beings attached to them. To acknowledge one's allegiance with or opposition to immigration issues will likely net the speaker a negative label for merely discussing the topic. Of course, such dissonance occurs among all races and cultures. The goal of this writing is to present a refractive thinking approach to addressing these undiscussables.

The academic environment should encourage open and honest dialogue with students and families (Sanders, 2012). For many faculty reading this chapter, we understand the hesitation to make the attempt at candor in broaching such a topic in conversation among colleagues or institutional leadership. We spend considerable time deep in thought to wordsmith conversations, sometimes to the point of absurdity, adding nothing of value or substance to discussions. Subsequently, we end up thwarting potential progress toward transitioning conversations into possible solutions.

Many faculty members who attempt to broach difficult topics often find themselves branded as racists or worse. The fallout is certainly not limited to professional educators. One need only to follow the news for examples of negative outcomes when journalists, politicians, or others make racially connected comments, take actions, or make seemingly innocent mistakes in the courses of their duties.

Former NFL player Colin Kaepernick's chose to *Take a Knee* during the playing of the National Anthem at football games to bring awareness to racial injustice suffered by African Americans (Yeboah, 2016). Kaepernick's protest not only cost him his job, but his kneeling inadvertently and incorrectly became a symbol of disrespect for the American flag and the U.S. military (Lowary, 2017). Maybe the misunderstanding that surrounded Kaepernick's actions were a result of misinformed people talking among themselves, rather than with Kaepernick or the diverse groups intended to be represented by the action.

Lisa Benson, an Emmy Award winning journalist with KSHB Kansas City, shared an article about White Fragility on her personal social media page and was subsequently terminated from her job (Steiner, 2017). The article touched on the idea that tears are a weapon White women use to silence or even eliminate women of color in professional and social settings. The anonymity afforded by social media allows users to speak more freely (Leetaru, 2018). Perhaps the electronic dissemination of the article was to avoid the potential defiance, judgement, or labeling that might accompany person-to-person discussion of racial topics such as White Fragility (Eddo-Lodge, 2017). Another undiscussable left undiscussed.

Another controversy continues with the longstanding immigration crisis along the southern border of the United States, which sparks rhetoric about the Dreamers and illegal immigrants and the quandary that surrounds their legal statuses in America. For anyone to openly declare their support of or opinion against them runs the risk of being labeled a variety of anti-border control, anti-American, unpatriotic, or racist against Hispanic or Latino people because of their decision to dare to speak openly about it.

Border security and immigration has been a longstanding point of contention in politics, business, education, and communities (Bryant, Triplett, & Watson, 2017). Demographic trends consistently indicated an increase in minority populations in American public schools, particularly Hispanic and Latino students (Bryant et al., 2017). More specifically, the National Center for Education Statistics (2019) reported an increase in the Hispanic student population from 16% to 26% from 2000–2015.

These changing demographics, regardless of the cause, persistently spurs conflict resulting in an *us against them* mindset that can affect assimilation or sense of belonging among Americans and Hispanic and Latino immigrants (Joshi, 2019). Politicians frequently strategize around this breach for political gain sometimes resulting in violence, division and racism (Joshi, 2019). A review of the national news currently illuminates these tensions in the United States today.

Former President Barack Obama's controversial Development, Relief, and Education for Alien Minors (DREAM) Act and Deferred Action for Childhood Arrivals (DACA) remain points of contention among the current administration. The DACA Act offered protection from deportation to undocumented immigrants who may have arrived in the United States very young where they had no control over coming here (Anti-Defamation League, 2019). The DREAM Act would have opened a pathway to become U.S. citizens for some undocumented immigrants who maintained clean records, attended college, or served in the military (Anti-Defamation League, 2019). Given the significant attention paid to immigration issues including these, the ability to discuss rationally these topics is critical if we, as a nation, hope to rectify them in a humane, safe, and equitable way.

The undiscussables surface when questions or comments about either perspective arise. To voice one's support of secure borders and tempered immigration can be twisted into what appears to be racist, separatist, anti-immigration rhetoric, particularly in the political arena.

To express support for immigration, DREAM or DACA could result in one being labeled unpatriotic, anti-American, or worse. The undiscussable rhetoric from the White House seems to fan the flames of division and even hate, specifically as related to borders and immigration.

President Donald Trump is vociferous of his inflammatory ideas on border safety and immigration. Ironically, even his most inappropriate utterances that for political or humane reasons may require immediate address are often rendered undiscussable by many within his administration. To discuss such matters could offer clarity and understanding of President Trump's intentions or ideas. When left unaddressed, listeners are left to run opaque information through their personal filters, which can, and has, had disastrous results. The *Unite the Right* political rally in Charlottesville, North Carolina stands as a prime example of how a lack of clear and open discussions can be devastating and destructive.

Those individuals who do not support President Trump's ideas are often vocal about their positions. However, among the Trump administration, Trump supporters, and select media outlets, Trump's most maligning statements remain defended and undiscussed. To openly criticize President Trump may render one a far left liberal, America-hater, or similar label. To openly support him may result in one being deemed one who passively agrees with President Trump's seemingly bigoted musings often reported in the media and his Twitter account.

The aforementioned statements are not meant to suggest President Trump is or is not anything other than President of the United States. Rather, the previous statements are meant to highlight political undiscussables related to immigration.

There are workable answers to these longstanding issues, however rational discussion is required to explore them. One's political preferences, personal views, or even conscious biases should not be sufficient to derail open, ethical, mature discussion about the lives, foreign and domestic, affected by our current immigration policies. In academia, the ability to discuss openly opposing views and ideas without fear of being misunderstood, misinterpreted, or labeled as a purveyor of hate is critical.

Faculty Issues

Often, faculty are dismissed for pandering personal philosophies and the content of the words they speak. The questions to consider carefully are whether faculty *truly* have free speech in the classroom or faculty meetings and whether they should. The casualty resulting from hindrances to free speech among faculty may not only affect civility but also leadership and leadership optics, begging the question, are these truly the results we want?

According to Quintana (2018), in an article for the Chronicle of Higher Education, Post Lecturer at Arcadia University and judicial political author Jeffrey Adam Sachs said, "faculty members are dismissed more often for liberal comments than conservative ones" (para. 1). Recently, the University of Oklahoma administration reached an impasse with an outspoken faculty member. Dr. Suzette Grillot, former Professor of International and Area Studies, who found herself in the hot seat for referencing public concerns related to free speech (Mangan, 2019). The impasse resulted in her being fired from her job.

There is no shortage of challenges to a supposedly free press. One only needs to Google *faculty under fire* and more than 95,000,000 results surface (May 12, 2019). Scandals related to free speech are plenteous from elementary schools to institutions of higher learning nationwide. A legitimate question is: What is really happening with free speech in academia?

Necessary but potentially controversial or sensitive dialogue seemingly can no longer occur in academia without serious fallout within the major and social medias or education administration. We cannot change what we cannot discuss, calmly, rationally, and with thoughtful consideration. When faculty cannot speak from the point of experience or observation, where does this leave our students and their educational experiences? How do we talk about the elephants in the room without the risk of public scolding, online harassment, being branded a racist, or being fired or worse? How can we prepare graduates to succeed in a diverse global environment when we cannot dialogue openly with others about what makes us alike as well as unique? Do we *really* value diversity as much as we say we do? As promoters of knowledge and opportunity, it is incumbent upon professional educators to highlight issues and increase awareness as the immigrant student population continues to increase, while concurrently facing a legislative push for results in educational accountability (Gonzalez, 2014).

The idea that faculty are fearful of speaking out on potentially controversial topics is not surprising. As professional educators, how do we model to our students how to gain knowledge and insight through dialogue if we ourselves play it safe and refrain from doing so? According to Pech and Durden (2004), many people believe that only those individuals at the top (in the C-Suite) possess such strategic literacy and management skills (as cited in Lentz, 2007), to address such controversy. Instead, all employees within the organization (from the bottom up) must possess these skills with which to steward an organization to serve the needs of those within it. We are all in this together.

Published in Sage Journals in 2018, Abby Ferber, member of Sociologists for Women in Society (SWS) dared to explore the problem of silencing faculty. Ferber offered a 20-point program to recommend changes that does not include hiding. Rather, Ferber's first point invites administrators to recognize the problem exists if there is any hope to move forward with correcting it.

Often, not *what* we say, but *how* we say it engenders respect or incites controversy. We often expect that professional educators should have the mastery to remain respectful and within the boundaries of rational behavior, when faced with elephants; those polarizing issues or hot topics that are potentially difficult, emotional, or politically charged when discussed. Identifying boundaries and rationality can be difficult as the goal posts are constantly moving depending on the topic and those individuals discussing it.

However, purposely sidestepping dialogue hinders forward progress toward solutions. In higher education, hiding does nothing to help us teach our students how to engage effectively with others.

Thus, the goal is to learn and model effective strategies of engaging in undiscussable discussions. We are scholars and members of the education community. We have a duty to prepare students to succeed personally and professionally among diverse peers, colleagues, and businesses. If not us, then who? If not now, then when?

Academic Freedom of Speech

Perlmutter (2019) offered an amusing commentary on language recommendations for individuals in positions of leadership. The irony may be reminiscent of the infamous line, "We are here to preserve democracy, not practice it," aptly stated in Richard Henrick's *Crimson Tide* (1994, p. 7). This commentary is similar for academics who may be the keepers of free speech, but are certainly constricted by its tenets (Perlmutter, 2019).

Eloquence by Perlmutter (2019) offers the following for contemplation:

> When you move into academic administration, you surrender your free-speech rights in many areas for legal, ethical, practical, and political reasons. Academic freedom, which you must defend vociferously for others, is constricted for you.
>
> Technology and social media ensures that all communications have an eternal presence in cyberspace. Administrators must be deliberate and reflective in their verbal and written dialogues, much more than faculty and others. (para 1 & 2)

Perlmutter offers pause for thought in looking at the goals of discussion. How can we strategically master the art of communication to not only approach difficult topics, but successfully solve the problems these topics put forth?

Let's practice the lessons of communication we teach in classes to our students by perhaps re-teaching them to our faculty. Should our focus be on our responses to such topics, rather than the questions? Perhaps tempered, genuine depersonalized responses could make broaching undiscussables easier. Perhaps checking one's motives for broaching an undiscussable could encourage transparent responses. Responsibility for meaningful effective dialogue about anything should be divided equally among all participants. There is no need to be fearful if we can discuss the undiscussables with respect and dignity. Emotional topics do not have to end in a barrage of tears, name-calling, or worse. We can and must learn to manage our emotions as we respectfully engage others if we are to reach the goal of effectively discussing the undiscussables.

Culture and Communities

The inability to discuss culture openly and honestly has its implications in communities as well as the classroom. Where in society is there a more diverse population than communities? As explained by City University of New York (2018), the idea of diversity refers to the respect and acceptance of all human characteristics in their social, cultural, historic, individual, and familial contexts. This includes ethnicity, gender, age, physical ability or disability, education, religion, immigration status, location, income, and even exposure to trauma (City University of New York, 2018).

Post-doctoral researcher Lotte Holck (2018) of the Copenhagen Business School posited that diversity in communities results in members who are more open-minded, value togetherness (coherence), and enjoy a deeper sense of well-being. These attributes could bring beauty and value to any community if all members cooperate and communicate with each other. Our collective resistance to discuss our cultural undiscussables portends to divide us indefinitely.

As mentioned earlier, journalist Lisa Benson Cooper, who is Black, shared the article *White Fragility* from her personal social media page and was fired from her job. According to Ganey, (2018), the article was offensive to two White colleagues resulting in Benson Cooper's termination for sharing it. The premise of the article is that White women use tears to silence or eliminate women of color in professional and social settings (Hamad, 2018). Many readers may have no idea of what Ruby Hamad, the author of *White Fragility,* was referring to. As a minority woman, one of the co-authors of this chapter knows exactly to what she referred. Her experience and observation were personal, not judgmental.

One of the authors of this chapter shares the following perspective: Having personally experienced the disconcerting tears of White women during discussions and the subsequent labels of being scary, aggressive, or intimidating because of those tears, the opportunity to discuss this phenomenon is appealing. In one workplace situation, the co-author involved pulled a White female coworker to the side after she, in a meeting of colleagues and supervisors, questioned competence related to an action the co-author had nothing to do with. While embarrassed in the meeting, the choice was to wait to address the matter later. The goal was to let her coworker know she was mistaken about the co-author's involvement in the action. Frank discussion took place; the coworker apologized for the mistake and the matter was seemingly put to rest.

Their mutual supervisor would later ask the co-author most gingerly if there were going to be any problems working with her colleague because she *frightened her* when she pulled her to the side. Apparently, she *burst into tears* in their supervisor's office after the 60-second discussion. Leaving the exchange with the supervisor emotionally rattled, the co-author pondered: "What was done to frighten her?" "What did my colleague say to our supervisor?" "What does our supervisor *really* think of me?" Protecting the White colleagues' feelings was the priority. No one ever asked for the co-author's side of the encounter or expressed any care for what the co-author might have been feeling afterward. This encounter was simply one of several over the years.

Our co-author would welcome an opportunity to sit with White women who have shed tears during discussions with her to get an understanding of what it is about her approach to them, or their beliefs about her as an individual that brought them to tears. Would not the ability to discuss their respective perspectives transparently without fear of possible repercussions been much more useful than both parties walking away with no more insight than before discussions began? We must create platforms where life's undiscussables can be openly and honestly discussed.

Political Undiscussables

The political stage offers opportunities to have meaningful conversations about undiscussables that need desperately to be discussed. The irony is that politicians often have the influence and authority to lead discussion of undiscussables but cannot or will not because the potential fallout for doing so could be career-ending. Political wisdom of old suggests politicians talking or campaigning about race is not a good idea (Bachman, 2018). However, Thompson (2018) suggested that some political parties continue to make drastic changes in the way they approach racial and cultural conversations.

Political topics that often generate emotional responses related to race and culture include the criminal justice system, education, immigration, border concerns, police-community relations, disparity in healthcare services, sexual orientation, and numerous other issues that influence politicians' approaches to voters. In our current political climate, we seem to experience a very polarized perspective on how to discuss the undiscussables that persistently plague society. Political scientists suggest candidates run a de-racialized campaign (Stout, 2018) to keep the loyalty of White voters (Thompson, 2018). Yet, politicians must hear the voices of voters of all colors as related to issues such as those aforementioned. It is not an option to sweep these elephants under the rug.

Conclusion

Reasons are numerous for not discussing the elephant in the room. Understandably, nobody wants to be misunderstood, misinterpreted, or labeled as a purveyor of hate. The undiscussables repeatedly surface when questions or comments about either side of a hot topic arise. Do faculty *truly* have free speech in the classroom, faculty meetings, or simply publicly voicing perspectives on issues that directly affect their work? It appears that necessary, but potentially controversial or sensitive dialogue can no longer occur in academia without serious fallout within the major and social medias or education administration. When faculty cannot speak from the point of experience or observation, where does this leave our students and their educational experiences? Immigration control and border safety has accentuated issues with the Dream Act and DACA. Immigrant students are filling our classrooms, and professional educators bear a tremendous responsibility for their learning. We are scholars and members of the education community. We have a duty to prepare students to succeed personally and professionally among diverse, peers, colleagues, and businesses. We cannot change what we cannot discuss, calmly, rationally, and with thoughtful consideration.

Actions taken by Kaepaernick and Benson demonstrate the severity of potential repercussions for broaching an undiscussable. President Trump's rhetoric has escalated racism, hatred, and bigoted musings. Could situations such as the *Unite the Right* political rally in Charlottesville, North Carolina been avoided by engaging in dialogue on sensitive topics? Is there a fine line between freedom of speech and undiscussable hot topics? On the political stage, it is compelling that undiscussable topics be discussed if we are to explore solutions to real problems as a society and a nation. Purposely sidestepping dialogue hinders forward progress toward solutions. Will potential consequences of avoiding the elephant in the room outweigh one over the other? Given the information in this chapter through the eyes of a refractive thinker, it is indeed a possibility.

THOUGHTS FROM THE ACADEMIC ENTREPRENEUR

The problem to be solved:

- Potentially sensitive topics are frequently off-limits for discussion, hindering opportunities for true cultural competency and value of diversity.

The goals:

- To create and maintain a climate that supports and encourages respectful, effective dialogue related to all manners of diversity.

The questions to ask:

- How can society work toward eliminating the negative labels assigned to inquirers that stifle meaningful dialogue around potentially sensitive or controversial issues?

- What can individuals and organizations do to collaborate and contribute to meaningful, effective conversations, openly and transparently, when discussing sensitive topics?Can cultural issues be overcome to create local teams for managing crises effectively?

Today's Business Application:

- Effective leaders who understand local cultures and know how to be effective despite differences are better equipped to respond successfully to natural disasters or human-induced crises.

- Preparation is fundamental to prevent or lessen the effects of crisis situations.

- Continuous communication inside and outside the organization will help leaders and crisis management teams resolve the crisis and lessen post-crisis effects.

REFERENCES

Anti-Defamation League. (2019). *What is DACA and who are the DREAMers?* Retrieved from http://www.adl.org

Bachman, J. (2018). *How a race-class narrative can work for Democrats.* Retrieved from https://www.theatlantic.com/politics/archive/2018/08/how-a-race-class-narrative-can-work-for-democrats/567185/

Bryant, A. C., Triplett, N. P., & Watson, M. J. (2017). Demographic trends indicate an increase in minority student populations in American public schools particularly Hispanics/Latino(a)s students. *Urban Review, 49*(2), 263–278. https://dx.doi.org/10.1007/s11256–017–0400–6

City University of New York. (n.d.). *Diversity and inclusion.* Retrieved from http://www2.cuny.edu/about/administration/offices/hr/diversity-and-recruitment/

Eddo-Lodge, R. (2017). *Why I'm no longer talking to white people about race.* Retrieved from http://www.theguardian.com

Ferber, A. L. (2018, May 4). "Are you willing to die for this work?": Public targeted online harassment. Higher *Education: SWS Presidential Address.* https://dx.doi.org/10.1177/0891243218766831

Ganey, J. (2018). *White women get Black reporter fired for sharing article on White privilege.* Retrieved from https://www.diversityinc.com/reporter-fired-sharing-white-tears/

Gonzalez, Y. L. (2014). *Improving Hispanic students' performance on science standardized tests: Successful practices from four elementary campuses* (Doctoral dissertation). Retrieved from ProQuest Dissertations and Theses database. (UMI No. 3583985)

Hamad, R. (2018). *How White women use tears to silence women of color.* Retrieved from https://www.theguardian.com/commentisfree/2018/may/08/how-white-women-use-strategic-tears-to-avoid-accountability

Hartsock, X. (2018). *How, why, and when to share your immigration status on job interviews.* Retrieved from https://www.fastcompany.com/40542890/how-why-and-when-to-share-your-immigration-status-on-job-interviews

Holcke, L. (2018). *Diversity leads to greater social coherence and well-being.* Retrieved from http://sciencenordic.com/diversity-leads-greater-social-coherence-and-well-being

Joshi, A. (2019). *Immigration, xenophobia and racism. Teaching global competence using the 2016 election.* Retrieved from https://asiasociety.org/education/immigration-xenophobia-and-racism

Leetaru, K. (2018). *Is social media empowering or silencing or voices?* Retrieved from http://www.Forbes.com

Lentz, C. (2007). *Strategic decision-making in organizational performance* (Doctoral dissertation). Retrieved from ProQuest Theses & Dissertations database. (UMI No. 3277192)

Lowary, J. (2017). What do veterans think about kneeling during the anthem? Views are diverse. Retrieved from USA Today Network via the Tennesean.com

Mangan, K. (2019, March 29). *Former U. of Oklahoma Dean sues president, provost, and university for bias, and free speech violation.* Retrieved from https://www.chronicle.com/article/Former-U-of-Oklahoma-Dean/246019

Perlmutter, D. D. (2019, January 2). *Administration 101: 4 phrases academic administrators should never say.* Retrieved from https://www.chronicle.com/article/Administration-101–4-Phrases/245364

Quintana, C. (2018, April 30). *The real free-speech crisis is professors being disciplined for liberal views a scholar finds.* Retrieved from https://www.chronicle.com/article/The-Real-Free-Speech-Crisis-Is/243284

Sanders, T. (2012). *A qualitative exploration of barriers to parental involvement in school activities among economically disadvantaged African American families* (Doctoral dissertation). Retrieved from ProQuest Dissertations and Theses Database.

Stout, C. (2018). *Black candidates know they have to be careful in talking about race. Here's what the research suggests.* Retrieved from https://www.washingtonpost.com/news/monkey-cage/wp/2019/02/19/black-candidates-know-they-have-to-be-careful-in-talking-about-race-heres-what-the-research-suggests/?noredirect=on&utm_term=.9f0b7d0525a4

Thompson, A. (2018). *Democrats are changing the way they talk about race.* Retrieved from https://www.politico.com/story/2018/11/19/democrats-2020-race-identity-politics-strategy-1000249

Yeboah, K. (2016). *A timeline of events since Colin Kaepernick's national anthem protest.* Retrieved from http://www.theundefeated.com.

About the Authors . . .

Dr. Yvonne L. Gonzalez earned a doctoral degree in Educational Leadership from the University of Phoenix in 2014. She has 19 years of experience in public education. Currently, Dr. Yvonne participates in a co-teaching model at the elementary level, providing bilingual, specialized curricular support to teachers and at-risk students. She has written curriculum for the school district where she is employed and facilitated district-wide professional development. Additionally, Dr. Yvonne has been an adjunct faculty member for the University of Phoenix since 2010.

Dr. Gonzalez reaches high levels of success with both teachers and students by engaging in meticulous data analysis and taking an inclusive approach to implementing a universal design for learning that works for all students.

To reach Dr. Gonzalez for additional information **e-mail: yvonne1615@ sbcglobal.net**

Dr. Teresa Sanders earned a doctoral degree in Educational Leadership from the University of Phoenix in 2007. She has 20 years of experience in mental health / social services and has been an educator for 13 years. Currently, Dr. Teresa teaches privately in a small, rural town in East Texas. Additionally, Dr. Teresa spent 12 years as an adjunct faculty member for the University of Phoenix.

Dr. Teresa works successfully with the most marginalized and challenging populations by taking a holistic, comprehensive approach to interacting with students and families and welcoming parents as allies in their children's education.

She is an education advocate for students and parents and believes for students to demonstrate maximum academic achievement, instruction must align with student's current academic ability, not necessarily grade level, and parents must be engaged actively in their children's schooling.

Dr. Teresa is an international best-selling author, has presented at four international education conferences, and writes weekly education columns for four newspapers. Dr. Teresa endeavors to develop a comprehensive education program to ensure students can read, write and complete basic math computations by the end of third grade.

To reach Dr. Sanders for additional information **e-mail:** TeresaEsanders@gmail.com

Dr. Cheryl Lentz is an international best-selling author, and keynote speaker, She holds a Doctor of Management Degree (DM) in Organizational Leadership, a Master of Science in International Relations from Troy University, and a Bachelor of Arts in Communication and Music History from the University of Illinois in Champaign, Urbana.

Dr. Cheryl, affectionately known as *Doc C* to her students, is a university professor of nearly 20 years, on faculty with Capella University, Embry-Riddle University, Grand Canyon University, and Walden University. Dr. Cheryl serves as a dissertation mentor / chair and committee member. She is also a dissertation coach, offering expertise as a professional editor for APA style for graduate thesis and doctoral dissertations, as well as faculty journal publications and books.

Awards include: Walden Faculty of the Year, DBA Program, 2016, UOP community service award, and 20 writing awards.

Dr. Cheryl is also an active member of Alpha Sigma Alpha Sorority.

She is a prolific author with more than 40 publications known for her writings on *The Golden Palace Theory of Management* and refractive thinking. Additional published works include her dissertation: *Strategic Decision Making in Organizational Performance, Journey Outside the Golden Palace, The Consumer Learner, Technology That Tutors, Effective Study Skills, The Dissertation Toolbox,* International Best Seller: *The Expert Success Solution,* and contributions to the award winning series: *The Refractive Thinker®: Anthology of Doctoral Learners, Volumes I-XVI.*

To reach Dr. Cheryl Lentz for information on refractive thinking, professional editing, radio show guest, or public speaking, please visit her **websites:** http://www.DrCherylLentz.com http://www.LentzLeadership.com or **e-mail:** drcheryllentz@gmail.com

Index

The Refractive Thinker®

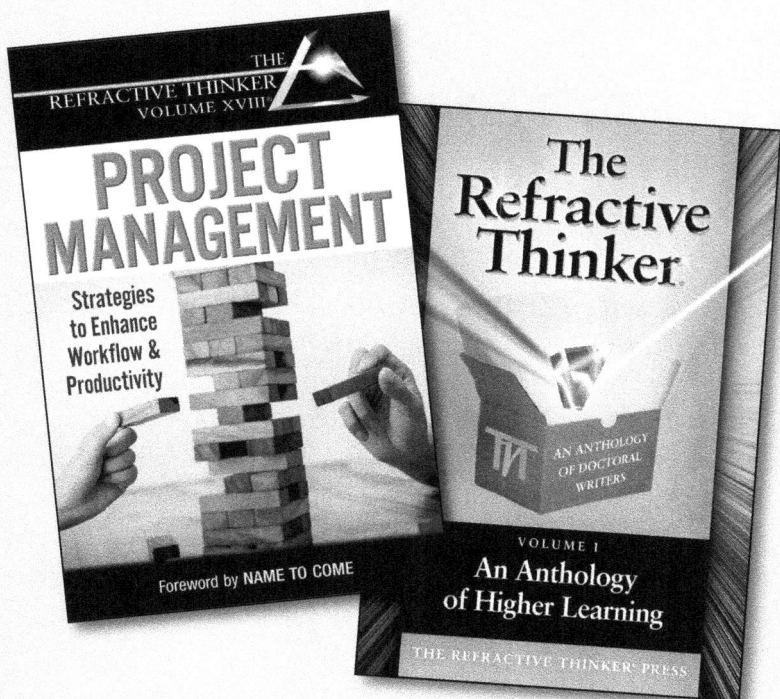

THE REFRACTIVE THINKER
VOLUME XVIII

PROJECT MANAGEMENT

Strategies to Enhance Workflow & Productivity

Foreword by NAME TO COME

The Refractive Thinker®

AN ANTHOLOGY OF DOCTORAL WRITERS

VOLUME I

An Anthology of Higher Learning

THE REFRACTIVE THINKER® PRESS

2019 CATALOG

The Refractive Thinker®:
An Anthology of Higher Learning

The Refractive Thinker® Press
info@refractivethinker.com
www.RefractiveThinker.com
blog: www.DissertationPublishing.com

Books are available through The Refractive Thinker® Press at special discounts for bulk purchases for the purpose of sales promotion, seminar attendance, or educational purposes. Special volumes can be created for specific purposes and to organizational specifications. Orders placed on www.RefractiveThinker.com for students and military receive a 15% discount. Please contact us for further details.

Refractive Thinker® logo by Joey Root; The Refractive Thinker® Press logo design by Jacqueline Teng, cover design by Peri Poloni-Gabriel, Knockout Design (knockoutbooks.com), cover design & production by Gary A. Rosenberg (thebookcouple.com).

I think therefore I am.
—Renee Descartes

I critically think to be.
I refractively think to change the world.

THANK YOU FOR JOINING US as we continue to celebrate the accomplishments of doctoral scholars affiliated with many phenomenal institutions of higher learning. The purpose of the anthology series is to share a glimpse into the scholarly works of participating authors on various subjects.

The Refractive Thinker® serves the tenets of leadership, which is not simply a concept outside of the self, but comes from within, defining our very essence; where the search to define leadership becomes our personal journey, not yet a finite destination.

The Refractive Thinker® is an intimate expression of who we are: the ability to think beyond the traditional boundaries of thinking and critical thinking. Instead of mere reflection and evaluation, one challenges the very boundaries of the constructs itself. If thinking is *inside* the box, and critical thinking is *outside* the box, we add the next step of refractive thinking, *beyond* the box. Perhaps the need exists to dissolve the box completely. The authors within these pages are on a mission to change the world. They are never satisfied or quite content with *what is* or asking *why,* instead these authors intentionally strive to push and test the limits to ask *why not.*

We look forward to your interest in discussing future opportunities. Let our collection of authors continue the journey initiated with Volume I, to which *The Refractive Thinker®* will serve as our guide to future volumes. Come join us in our quest to be refractive thinkers and add your wisdom to the collective. We look forward to your stories.

Please contact The Refractive Thinker® Press for information regarding these authors and the works contained within these pages. Perhaps you or your organization may be looking for an author's expertise to incorporate as part of your annual corporate meetings as a keynote or guest speaker(s), perhaps to offer individual, or group seminars or coaching, or require their expertise as consultants.

Join us on our continuing adventures of *The Refractive Thinker*® where we expand the discussion specifically begun in Volume I: Leadership; Volume II (Editions 1–3): Research Methodology; Volume III: Change Management; Volume IV: Ethics, Leadership, and Globalization; Volume V: Strategy in Innovation; Volume VI: Post-Secondary Education; Volume VII: Social Responsibility; Volume VIII: Effective Business Practices in Motivation & Communication; Volume IX: Effective Business Practices in Leadership & Emerging Technologies; Volume X: Effective Business Strategies for the Defense Industry Sector; Volume XI: Women in Leadership; Volume XII: Cybersecurity in an Increasingly Insecure World; Volume XIV: Healthcare; Volume XV: Nonprofits; and Volume XVI: Generations: Strategies for Managing Generations in the Workforce. All our volumes are themed to explore the realm of strategic thought, creativity, and innovation.

Dr. Cheryl A. Lentz, managing editor of The Lentz Leadership Institute, explains the unique benefits of the books for readers:

"They celebrate the diffusion of innovative refractive thinking through the writings of these doctoral scholars as they dare to think differently in search of new applications and understandings of research. Unlike most academic books that merely define research, The Refractive Thinker® *offers unique applications of research from the perspective of multiple authors—each offering a chapter based on their specific expertise."*

THE REFRACTIVE THINKER® PRESS

Refractive Thinker volumes are available in e-book, Kindle®, iPad®, Nook®, and Sony Reader™, as well as individual e-chapters by author.

COMING SOON FROM THE REFRACTIVE THINKER®!
AVAILABLE THRU THE LENTZ LEADERSHIP INSTITUTE
The Refractive Thinker®: Vol XVIII: Project Management

Telephone orders: Call us at 702.719.9214

Email Orders: drcheryllentz@gmail.com

Website orders: Please place orders through our website:
www.RefractiveThinker.com

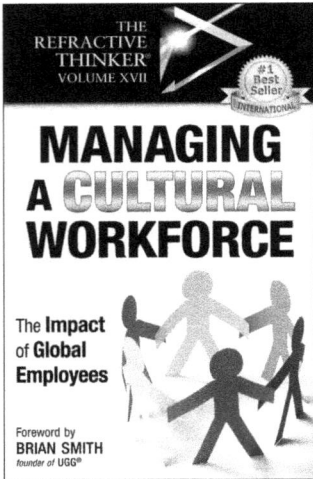

#1 Amazon Best Seller!
Next Generation Indie Finalist 2019
Gold & Silver eLit Awards 2019

The Refractive Thinker®: Volume XIV:
Health Care: The Impact on Leadership,
Business, and Education

Dr. Gladys Taylor McGarey is internationally known for her pioneer work in alternative medicine. She believes that the practice of medicine has become a war against disease, a killing machine. Her premise is that we must change our focus from killing to living. As we support the living process in a person, life itself brings about the healing that the person needs. Our job as physicians is to work and support the 'Physician Within' each of us.

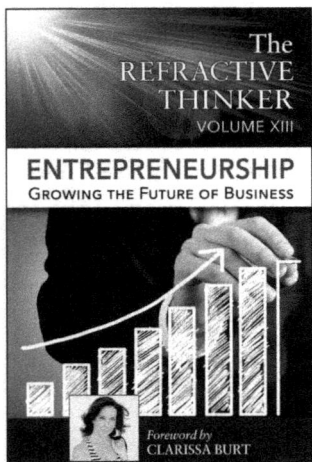

The Refractive Thinker®: Volume XIII:
Entrepreneurship: Growing the Future
of Business

Join Clarissa Burt and contributing scholars as they discuss current research regarding the future of business and the influence of the entrepreneur. This volume contains research on what the future may hold to success of the economy in the hands of the emerging and evolving small business owner and entrepreneur. As you read, ask yourself: "What should I be doing as an entrepreneur to contribute to the world economy as well as my own success?"

For more information, please visit our website: www.RefractiveThinker.com

PUBLICATIONS ORDER FORM

PLEASE SEND THE FOLLOWING BOOKS FROM THE REFRACTIVE THINKER®:

- ❏ *Volume I: An Anthology of Higher Learning*
- ❏ *Volume II: Research Methodology*
- ❏ *Volume II: Research Methodology, 2nd Edition*
- ❏ *Volume II: Research Methodology, 3rd Edition*
- ❏ *Volume III: Change Management*
- ❏ *Volume IV: Ethics, Leadership, and Globalization*
- ❏ *Volume V: Strategy in Innovation*
- ❏ *Volume VI: Post-Secondary Education*
- ❏ *Volume VII: Social Responsibility*
- ❏ *Volume VIII: Effective Business Practices*
- ❏ *Volume IX: Effective Business Practices in Leadership & Emerging Technologies*
- ❏ *Volume X: Effective Business Strategies for the Defense Industry Sector*
- ❏ *Volume XI: Women in Leadership*
- ❏ *Volume XII: Cybersecurity*
- ❏ *Volume XIII: Entrepreneurship*
- ❏ *Volume XIV: Healthcare*
- ❏ *Volume XV: Nonprofits*
- ❏ *Volume XVI: Generations*

Please contact the Refractive Thinker® Press for book prices, e-book prices, and shipping. Individual e-chapters available by author: $3.95 (plus applicable tax). www.RefractiveThinker.com

- ❏ *So You Think You Can Edit?*
- ❏ *The Expert Success Solution*
- ❏ *The Unbounded Dimensions Series*
- ❏ *Ethics, Employment Law, and Faith-Based Universities*
- ❏ *Effective Study Skills in 5 Simple Steps*
- ❏ *Technology That Tutors*
- ❏ *Siberian Husky Rescue*
- ❏ *The Consumer Learner*
- ❏ *Journey Outside the Golden Palace*
- ❏ *The Dissertation Toolbox*

PLEASE SEND MORE FREE INFORMATION:

❏ Speaking engagements ❏ Educational seminars ❏ Consulting

JOIN OUR MAILING LIST:

Name: _____

Address: _____

City: _____ State: _____ Zip: _____

Telephone: _____ Email: _____

E-MAIL FORM TO: The Refractive Thinker® Press: drcheryllentz@gmail.com

Participation in Future Volumes of
The Refractive Thinker®

Yes, I would like to participate in:

❏ **Doctoral Volume**(s) for a specific university or organization:

Name: _____

Contact Person: _____

Telephone: _____ E-mail: _____

❏ **Specialized Volume**(s) Business or Themed:

Name: _____

Contact Person: _____

Telephone: _____ E-mail: _____

E-MAIL FORM TO: THE REFRACTIVE THINKER® PRESS
drcheryllentz@gmail.com
www.RefractiveThinker.com

Join us on Twitter, LinkedIn, and Facebook